Multiculturalism

✣

Multiculturalism

EXAMINING THE POLITICS
OF RECOGNITION

✣

CHARLES TAYLOR

K. ANTHONY APPIAH
JÜRGEN HABERMAS
STEVEN C. ROCKEFELLER
MICHAEL WALZER
SUSAN WOLF

Edited and Introduced by AMY GUTMANN

PRINCETON UNIVERSITY PRESS

PRINCETON, NEW JERSEY

Library of Congress Cataloging-in-Publication Data

Multiculturalism: examining the politics of recognition /
Charles Taylor . . . [et al.]; edited and introduced by Amy Gutmann.
p.   cm.
Expanded ed. of: Multiculturalism and "The politics of recognition" /
Charles Taylor. c1992.
Includes bibliographical references and index.
ISBN 0-691-03779-5 (PA)
1. Multiculturalism—United States.   2. Multiculturalism.
3. Minorities—United States—Political activity.   4. Minorities—
Political activity.   5. Political culture—United States.
6. Political culture.   I. Taylor, Charles, 1931–   .
II. Gutmann, Amy.   III. Taylor, Charles, 1931–   Multiculturalism
and "The politics of recognition."
E184.A1M84   1994
305.8'00973—dc20   94-19602

This book has been composed in Linotron Palatino

Printed in the United States of America

17   19   20   18   16

ISBN-13: 978-0-691-03779-0 (pbk.)

FOR LAURANCE S. ROCKEFELLER

✣

❖ *Contents* ❖

⁖ *Preface (1994)* ⁖

SINCE its publication in 1992, *Multiculturalism and "The Politics of Recognition"* has appeared in Italian, French, and German editions. The German edition includes an extended commentary by the political philosopher Jürgen Habermas, who adds an important voice to a now-multinational discussion about the relationship between constitutional democracy and a politics that recognizes diverse cultural identities. We invited K. Anthony Appiah, Professor of Afro-American Studies and Philosophy at Harvard, to offer his reflections on the politics of recognition. Appiah has written a rich essay on the problematic relationship between recognition of collective identities, the ideal of individual authenticity, and the survival of cultures. We are pleased to be able to include both essays in this expanded edition.

Drawing on a Kantian perspective, Habermas argues that equal protection under the law is not enough to constitute a constitutional democracy. We must not only be equal under the law, we must also be able to understand ourselves as the authors of the laws that bind us. "Once we take this internal connection between democracy and the constitutional state seriously," Habermas writes, "it becomes clear that the system of rights is blind neither to unequal social conditions nor to cultural differences." What count as equal rights for women or for ethnic and cultural minorities cannot even be understood adequately until members of these groups "articulate and justify in public discussion what is relevant to equal or unequal treatment in typical cases." Democratic discussions also enable citizens to clarify "which traditions they want to perpetuate and which they want to discontinue, how they want to deal with their history, with one another, with nature, and so on." Constitutional democracy can thrive on the conflict generated by these discussions and live well with their democratic resolutions, Habermas suggests, as long as citizens are united by mutual respect for others' rights.

Habermas distinguishes between culture, broadly understood, which need not be shared by all citizens, and a common *political* culture marked by mutual respect for rights. Constitutional democracy dedicates itself to this distinction by granting members of minority cultures "equal rights of coexistence" with majority cultures. Are these group rights or individual rights? Habermas maintains that they are individual rights of free association and nondiscrimination, which therefore do not guarantee survival for any culture. The political project of preserving cultures as if they were endangered species deprives cultures of their vitality and individuals of their freedom to revise and even to reject their inherited cultural identities. Constitutional democracies respect a broad range of cultural identities, but they guarantee survival to none.

Appiah's essay provides further reason to worry about the demand for cultural survival understood as a political guarantee that any culture continue to exist through indefinite future generations. Appiah agrees with Taylor that there are "legitimate collective goals whose pursuit will require giving up pure proceduralism," but indefinite cultural survival is not among those goals. In explaining why, Appiah gives voice to the ideal of individual autonomy, exploring its uneasy relationship with collective identity.

Appiah asks us to worry about the fact that collective identities—the identification of people as members of a particular gender, race, ethnicity, nationality, or sexuality—"come with notions of how a proper person of that kind behaves: it is not that there is *one* way that gays or blacks should behave, but that there are gay and black modes of behavior." Personal dimensions of identity—being witty, wise, and caring—do not typically work in the same way as the collective dimensions. The collective dimensions, Appiah writes, "provide what we might call scripts: narratives that people can use in shaping their life plans and in telling their life stories. In our society (though not, perhaps, in the England of Addison and Steele) being witty does not in this way suggest the life-script of 'the wit.'"

The life-scripts associated with women, homosexuals, blacks, Catholics, Jews, and various other collective identities have often been negative, creating obstacles to, rather than opportunities for, living a socially dignified life and being treated as equals by other members of their society. The demand for political recognition might be viewed as a way of revising the inherited social meaning of their identities, of constructing positive life scripts where there once were primarily negative ones. "It may even be historically, strategically necessary, " Appiah speculates, "for the story to go this way." But, he immediately adds, anyone who takes autonomy seriously should not be satisfied were the story to end this way, for would we not have then "replaced one kind of tyranny with another"? Is the strategic virtue of a politics of recognition not also a vice from the perspective of individual autonomy? Appiah rejects group recognition as an ideal because it ties individuals too tightly to scripts over which they have too little authorial control. "The politics of recognition," Appiah worries, "requires that one's skin color, one's sexual body, should be acknowledged politically in ways that make it hard for those who want to treat their skin and their sexual body as personal dimensions of the self. And personal means not secret, but not too tightly scripted."

Can there be a politics of recognition that respects a multitude of multicultural identities and does not script too tightly any one life? Both Appiah and Habermas offer complex answers to this question, pointing to the possibility that some form of constitutional democracy may offer such a politics, based not on class, race, ethnicity, gender, or nationality, but rather on a democratic citizenship of equal liberties, opportunities, and responsibilities for individuals.

Amy Gutmann
March 25, 1994

❖ *Preface and Acknowledgments* ❖

THIS VOLUME was first conceived to mark the inauguration of the University Center for Human Values at Princeton University. Founded in 1990, the University Center supports teaching, research, and public discussions of fundamental questions concerning moral values that span traditional academic disciplines. Central among those questions is what kind of communities can justly be created and sustained out of our human diversity. Unprecedented powers of creation and destruction are at the disposal of increasingly interdependent societies, with remarkably diverse cultures, governments, and religions. Colleges and universities like Princeton have themselves become increasingly pluralistic communities. Accompanying this pluralism is a widespread skepticism about the defensibility of any moral principles or perspectives. Many moral problems are upon us, and many people question our ability to deal with them in a reasonable way.

The ethical issues of our time pose a challenge to any university committed to an educational mission that encompasses more than the development and dissemination of empirical knowledge and technical skills. Can people who differ in their moral perspectives nonetheless reason together in ways that are productive of greater ethical understanding? The University Center faces up to this challenge by supporting a university education that is centrally concerned with examining ethical values, the various standards according to which individuals and groups make significant choices and evaluate their own as well as other ways of life. Through the teaching, research, and public discussions that it sponsors, the University Center encourages the systematic study of ethical values and the mutual influences of education, phi-

losophy, religion, politics, the professions, the arts, literature, science and technology, and ethical life. In no small
part, the promise of ethical understanding lies in its educational practice. If universities are not dedicated to pushing
our individual and collective reasoning about human values
to its limits, then who will be?

Many dedicated people contributed to creating the University Center, more than I can mention here. But a few people
deserve special thanks. When Harold T. Shapiro delivered
his Inaugural Address as eighteenth President of Princeton
University in 1988, he focused on the importance of the university's role in encouraging ethical inquiry, "not to proclaim
a set of doctrines for society, but rather to ensure that students and faculty keep the important problems of our humanity before us—and always keep up the search for alternatives." President Shapiro carried through on his words in
supporting the University Center.

It has been my great pleasure to work with a group of su-
perb scholars and teachers from many different disciplines
who have directly shaped the University Center and indi-
rectly shaped this volume. Central among them are John
Cooper, George Kateb, Alexander Nehamas, Albert Rabo-
teau, Alan Ryan, Jeffrey Stout, and Robert Wuthnow, all
members of the University Center's executive committee
who worked collaboratively for countless hours to create the
University Center. Helen Nissenbaum, the Associate Director, joined the University Center just in time to oversee plan-
ning for the Inaugural Lecture. She has also contributed in
invaluable ways in shaping this volume from start to finish.
Valerie Kanka, Assistant in the University Center, carried
through on countless details with great verve and commitment.

On behalf of everyone who has contributed to creating the
University Center and everyone who will benefit from its
creation, I thank Laurance S. Rockefeller, Princeton Class of

1932, whose generosity and vision have made the University Center possible. We dedicate this inaugural volume to him.

Amy Gutmann
Director, University Center for Human Values

PART ONE

✣

‡

Introduction

AMY GUTMANN

Public institutions, including government agencies, schools, and liberal arts colleges and universities, have come under severe criticism these days for failing to recognize or respect the particular cultural identities of citizens. In the United States, the controversy most often focuses upon the needs of African-Americans, Asian-Americans, Native Americans, and women. Other groups could easily be added to this list, and the list would change as we moved around the world. Yet it is hard to find a democratic or democratizing society these days that is not the site of some significant controversy over whether and how its public institutions should better recognize the identities of cultural and disadvantaged minorities. What does it mean for citizens with different cultural identities, often based on ethnicity, race, gender, or religion, to recognize ourselves as equals in the way we are treated in politics? In the way our children are educated in public schools? In the curricula and social policy of liberal arts colleges and universities?

This volume focuses on the challenge of multiculturalism and the politics of recognition as it faces democratic societies today, particularly the United States and Canada, although the basic moral issues are similar in many other democracies. The challenge is endemic to liberal democracies because they are committed in principle to equal representation of all. Is a democracy letting citizens down, excluding or discriminating against us in some morally troubling way, when major institutions fail to take account of our particular identities? Can citizens with diverse identities be represented as equals if

3

public institutions do not recognize our particular identities, but only our more universally shared interests in civil and political liberties, income, health care, and education? Apart from ceding each of us the same rights as all other citizens, what does respecting people as equals entail? In what sense should our identities as men or women, African-Americans, Asian-Americans, or Native Americans, Christians, Jews, or Muslims, English or French Canadians *publicly* matter?

One reasonable reaction to questions about how to recognize the distinct cultural identities of members of a pluralistic society is that the very aim of representing or respecting differences in public institutions is misguided. An important strand of contemporary liberalism lends support to this reaction. It suggests that our lack of identification with institutions that serve public purposes, the impersonality of public institutions, is the price that citizens should be willing to pay for living in a society that treats us all as equals, regardless of our particular ethnic, religious, racial, or sexual identities. It is the neutrality of the public sphere, which includes not only government agencies but also institutions like Princeton and other liberal universities, that protects our freedom and equality as citizens. On this view, our freedom and equality as citizens refer only to our common characteristics—our universal needs, regardless of our particular cultural identities, for "primary goods" such as income, health care, education, religious freedom, freedom of conscience, speech, press, and association, due process, the right to vote, and the right to hold public office. These are interests shared by almost all people regardless of our particular race, religion, ethnicity, or gender. And therefore public institutions need not—indeed should not—strive to recognize our particular cultural identities in treating us as free and equal citizens.

Can we then conclude that all of the demands for recognition by particular groups, often made in the name of nationalism or multiculturalism, are *illiberal* demands? This conclusion is surely too hasty. We need to ask more about the requirements of treating people as free and equal citizens. Do most people need a secure cultural context to give meaning and guidance to their choices in life? If so, then a secure cultural context also ranks among the primary goods, basic to most people's prospects for living what they can identify as a good life. And liberal democratic states are obligated to help disadvantaged groups preserve their culture against intrusions by majoritarian or "mass" cultures. Recognizing and treating members of some groups as equals now seems to require public institutions to acknowledge rather than ignore cultural particularities, at least for those people whose self-understanding depends on the vitality of their culture. This requirement of political recognition of cultural particularity— extended to all individuals—is compatible with a form of universalism that counts the culture and cultural context valued by individuals as among their basic interests.

We encounter problems, however, once we look into the *content* of the various valued cultures. Should a liberal democratic society respect those cultures whose attitudes of ethnic or racial superiority, for example, are antagonistic to other cultures? If so, how can respect for a culture of ethnic or racial superiority be reconciled with the commitment to treating all people as equals? If a liberal democracy need not or should not respect such "supremacist" cultures, even if those cultures are highly valued by many among the disadvantaged, what precisely are the moral limits on the legitimate demand for political recognition of particular cultures?

Questions concerning whether and how cultural groups should be recognized in politics are among the most salient and vexing on the political agenda of many democratic and democratizing societies today. Charles Taylor offers an original perspective on these problems in "The Politics of Recognition," based upon his Inaugural Lecture for the University Center for Human Values at Princeton University.

Taylor steps back from the political controversies that rage over nationalism, feminism, and multiculturalism to offer a historically informed, philosophical perspective on what is at stake in the demand made by many people for recognition of their particular identities by public institutions. In the ancien régime, when a minority could count on being honored (as "Ladies" and "Lords") and the majority could not realistically aspire to public recognition, the demand for recognition was unnecessary for the few and futile for the many. Only with the collapse of stable social hierarchies does the demand for public recognition become commonplace, along with the idea of the dignity of all individuals. Everyone is an equal—a Mr., Miss, Mrs., or Ms.—and we all expect to be recognized as such. So far, so good.

But the claims of equal citizens in the public sphere are more problematic and conflict-ridden than our appreciation of the collapse of aristocratic honor would lead us to expect. Taylor highlights the problems in the ingenious attempt by Jean-Jacques Rousseau and his followers to satisfy the perceived universal need for public recognition by converting human equality into identity. The Rousseauean politics of recognition, as Taylor characterizes it, is simultaneously suspicious of all social differentiation and receptive to the homogenizing—indeed even totalitarian—tendencies of a politics of *the* common good, where the common good reflects the universal identity of all citizens. The demand for recognition may be satisfied on this scheme, but only after it has been socially and politically disciplined so that people pride themselves on being little more than equal citizens and therefore expect to be publicly recognized *only* as such. Taylor rightly argues that this is too high a price to pay for the politics of recognition.

Liberal democracies, *pace* Rousseau, cannot regard citizenship as a comprehensive universal identity because (1) people are unique, self-creating, and creative individuals, as John Stuart Mill and Ralph Waldo Emerson famously recognized; and (2) people are also "culture-bearing," and the cultures they bear differ depending on their past and present

6

identifications. The unique, self-creating, and creative conception of human beings is not to be confused with a picture of "atomistic" individuals creating their identities *de novo* and pursuing their ends independently of each other. Part of the uniqueness of individuals results from the ways in which they integrate, reflect upon, and modify their own cultural heritage and that of other people with whom they come into contact. Human identity is created, as Taylor puts it, *dialogically*, in response to our relations, including our actual dialogues, with others. The dichotomy posed by some political theorists between atomistic and socially constructed individuals is therefore a false one. If human identity is dialogically created and constituted, then public recognition of our identity requires a politics that leaves room for us to deliberate publicly about those aspects of our identities that we share, or potentially share, with other citizens. A society that recognizes individual identity will be a deliberative, democratic society because individual identity is partly constituted by collective dialogues.

Granting the totalitarian tendency of the Rousseauean quest for a politics that comprehensively recognizes the identity of citizens, Taylor argues that public institutions should not—indeed cannot—simply refuse to respond to the demand for recognition by citizens. The anti-Rousseauean demand to be publicly recognized for one's *particularity* is also as understandable as it is problematic and controversial. We disagree, for example, as to whether in the name of human equality and treating all people as equals society should treat women the same way that it treats men, considering pregnancy as another form of physical disability, or differently in recognition of those aspects of our identities that are distinctly tied to gender, such as the social identity of most American women as child-bearers and primary child-rearers. We disagree as to whether African-American students are better served by public schools with a curriculum specially designed to emphasize African-American culture or by a curriculum that is common to all students. The demand for recognition, animated by the ideal of human dignity, points in at least two directions, both to the protection of the basic rights of individuals as human beings and to the acknowledgment of the particular needs of individuals as members of specific cultural groups. Because Taylor takes seriously the stakes on both sides of the controversy, he does not jump aboard any political bandwagon, or offer simple solutions where there are none.

Nor do Susan Wolf, Steven C. Rockefeller, and Michael Walzer, who in commenting on Taylor's essay suggest new ways of conceiving the relationship between our personal identities and our political practices. Wolf focuses on the challenges of feminism and multicultural education. Although the situation of women is often compared to that of disadvantaged cultural minorities, Wolf suggests that there is a critical distinction between the two cases. Whereas political recognition of the distinctive contributions and qualities of minority cultures is most often viewed as a way of treating members of those cultures as equals, political recognition of the distinctiveness of women as women is typically identified with regarding women as unequals, and expecting (or even requiring) women to stay in distinctively "feminine" and subordinate places in society. And yet the demand for public recognition by women is in another significant way similar to the demand made by many minorities. Full public recognition as equal citizens may require two forms of respect: (1) respect for the unique identities of each individual, regardless of gender, race, or ethnicity, and (2) respect for those activities, practices, and ways of viewing the world that are particularly valued by, or associated with, members of disadvantaged groups, including women, Asian-Americans, African-Americans, Native Americans, and a multitude of other groups in the United States.

Steven C. Rockefeller rightly worries about the abuse of the second requirement, respect for individuals as they identify with particular cultural groups. If members of groups are *publicly* identified with the dominant characteristics, practices, and values of their group, one might wonder whether our particular identities—as English or French Canadians, men or women, Asian-Americans, African-Americans, or Native Americans, Christians, Jews, or Muslims—will take public precedence over our more universal identity as persons, deserving of mutual respect, civil and political liberties, and decent life chances simply by virtue of our equal humanity. Recognition of every individual's uniqueness and humanity lies at the core of liberal democracy, understood as a way of political and personal life. The liberal democratic value of diversity therefore may not be captured by the need to preserve distinct and unique cultures over time, which provide each separate group of people with a secure culture and identity for themselves and their progeny. Rockefeller follows John Dewey in connecting the democratic value of diversity instead with the value of expanding the cultural, intellectual, and spiritual horizons of all individuals, enriching our world by exposing us to differing cultural and intellectual perspectives, and thereby increasing our possibilities for intellectual and spiritual growth, exploration, and enlightenment.

Does this liberal democratic view downplay the human need for secure and separate cultural identities? It is probably impossible to say with any certainty in light of the relatively few developed democracies in our world. So for the sake of challenging this democratic vision, we might suppose that its ideal of individuals flourishing in a mobile, multicultural society (or world) does indeed underestimate the need of people as members of discrete ethnic, linguistic, and other cultural groups for public recognition and preservation of their particular cultural identities. Even in light of this challenge, the liberal democratic view offers a morally significant and politically useful antidote to the demand for cultural recognition as it is now commonly made on behalf of

distinct groups. Liberal democracy is suspicious of the demand to enlist politics in the preservation of separate group
identities or the survival of subcultures that otherwise would
not flourish through the free association of citizens. And yet
democratic institutions, more than any others, tend to expose citizens to a diverse set of cultural values. Hence liberal
democracy enriches our opportunities, enables us to recognize the value of various cultures, and thereby teaches us to
appreciate diversity not simply for its own sake but for its
enhancement of the quality of life and learning. The liberal
democratic defense of diversity draws upon a universalistic
rather than a particularistic perspective.

What exactly is the universalistic perspective with which
liberal democracy views and values multiculturalism? Building on Taylor's analysis, Walzer suggests that there may not
be one universalistic perspective, but two, which pull liberal
democracies in different political directions. Or, more accurately, there is one universalistic principle, widely accepted
by people who broadly believe in human equality and in-
completely institutionalized in liberal democratic societies:
"Treat all people as free and equal beings." But there are two
plausible and historically influential interpretations of this
principle. One perspective requires political neutrality
among the diverse and often conflicting conceptions of the
good life held by citizens of a pluralistic society. The paradigm of this perspective is the American doctrine of separation of church and state, where the state not only protects
the religious freedom of all citizens but also avoids as far as
possible identifying any of its own institutions with a particular religious tradition.

The second liberal democratic perspective, also universalistic, does not insist on neutrality for either the consequences
or the justification of public policies, but rather permits public institutions to further particular cultural values on three
conditions: (1) the basic rights of all citizens—including freedom of speech, thought, religion, and association—must be

protected, (2) no one is manipulated (and of course not coerced) into accepting the cultural values that are represented
by public institutions, and (3) the public officials and institutions that make cultural choices are democratically accountable, not only in principle but also in practice. The paradigm
of this perspective is democratic subsidy for, and control
over, education in the United States. At the same time that
our constitution requires separation of church and state, it
grants states wide latitude in determining the cultural content of children's education. Educational policy in America,
far from requiring neutrality, encourages local communities
to shape schools partly in their particular cultural image, so
long as they do not violate basic rights, such as freedom of
conscience or the separation of church and state.

Walzer sees the two universalistic perspectives as defining
two different conceptions of liberalism, the second more
democratic than the first. What Walzer calls "Liberalism 2,"
inasmuch as it authorizes democratic communities to determine public policy within the broad limits of respect for individual rights, also authorizes them to choose policies that
are, more or less, neutral among the particular cultural identities of groups. Because Liberalism 2 is democratic, it can
choose Liberalism 1, state neutrality, through a democratic
consensus. Walzer thinks this is what the United States has
democratically chosen. And Liberalism 1 chosen within Liberalism 2 is what Walzer would choose, because it is in keep-
ing with the dominant social understanding of the United
States as a society of immigrants, where each cultural group
is free to fend for itself, but not to enlist the state in support
or recognition of its particular cultural projects.

When I listen to the discordant voices raised in recent debates over multiculturalism, I find it hard to say what we as
a society have chosen, at least at this level of abstraction.
Apart from the difficult, perhaps inescapable, problem of fig-
uring out what "we" have chosen, perhaps it is a mistake to
think that we have chosen, or need to choose, one liberalism

or the other for *all* of our public institutions and policies. Perhaps the two universalisms are better interpreted not as two distinct and politically comprehensive conceptions of liberalism but as two strands of a single conception of liberal democracy that recommends—indeed occasionally even requires—state neutrality in certain realms such as religion, but not in others, such as education, where democratically accountable institutions are free to reflect the values of one or more cultural communities as long as they also respect the basic rights of all citizens. The dignity of free and equal beings requires liberal democratic institutions to be nonrepressive, nondiscriminatory, and deliberative. These principled constraints leave room for public institutions to recognize the particular cultural identities of those they represent. This conclusion identifies liberal democracy at its best with *both* the protection of universal rights and public recognition of particular cultures, although for significantly different reasons from those that Taylor recommends. The results of democratic deliberations consistent with respect for individuals' rights (freedom of speech, religion, press, association, and so on), not the survival of subcultures, come to the defense of multiculturalism.

Along with Taylor's essay, the comments of Wolf, Rockefeller, and Walzer are intended to stimulate more constructive discussions of the issues surrounding multiculturalism than those that now dominate public discourse. In that same spirit, we might also consider here the debate over multiculturalism closer to home, the public controversy over multiculturalism that has hit the campuses of American colleges and universities, where we have witnessed some of the most acrimonious arguments. Even though life and death do not hang on the outcome, the political identity of Americans, the quality of our collective intellectual life, and the nature and value of higher education are all at issue. So the stakes are rightly perceived as high. Consider the opening lines of an op-ed piece that ran in the *Wall Street Journal* in the midst of the controversy that raged over Stanford University's core curriculum: "The intellectual heritage of the West goes on trial at Stanford University today. Most predict it will lose." The controversy referred to by the author of the piece, Isaac Barchas, a Stanford classics major, revolved around the content of Stanford's only year-long requirement in "Western Culture." Students were required to choose one of eight courses, all of which shared a core reading list of fifteen works by classical thinkers such as Plato, Homer, Dante, and Darwin.

If Barchas's characterization is correct, the intellectual heritage of the West lost at Stanford three years ago, with remarkably little opposition from the faculty. The faculty voted, 39 to 4, to replace the requirement in Western Culture with one called "Culture, Ideas, and Values" that adds works of some non-European cultures and works by women, African-Americans, Hispanics, Asians, and Native Americans to a contracted core of the classics. The Old and New Testament, Plato, Saint Augustine, Machiavelli, Rousseau, and Marx remain in the new core.

In the ensuing public debate over whether to change the content of such core courses, one side—call them "essentialists"—argued that to dilute the core with new works for the sake of including previously unheard voices would be to forsake the values of Western civilization for the standardlessness of relativism, the tyranny of the social sciences, lightweight trendiness, and a host of related intellectual and political evils. Another, diametrically opposed side—call them "deconstructionists"—argued that to preserve the core by excluding contributions to civilization by women, African-Americans, Hispanics, Asians, and Native Americans as if the classical canon were sacred, unchanging, and unchangeable would be to denigrate the identities of members of these previously excluded groups and to close off Western civilization from the influences of unorthodox and challenging ideas for the sake of perpetuating sexism, racism, Eurocentrism, closed-mindedness, the tyranny of Truth (with a capital "T"), and a host of related intellectual and political evils.

Much more is at issue, and of value, here than meets the ear in the public debate between essentialists and deconstructionists. If the intellectual heritage of the West went on trial at Stanford and other campuses that have considered changing their core curricula, then the intellectual heritage of the West lost before the trials began. Neither the intellectual heritage of the West nor the liberal democratic ideal of higher education can be preserved by a decision to require or not to require of every university student several courses in fifteen, thirty, or even a hundred great books. Nor can our heritage be eradicated by a decision to decrease the number of canonical books to make room for newer, less established, less widely esteemed or even less lasting works that speak more explicitly to the experiences or better express the sense of social alienation of women and minorities. The reason is not that Western civilization will not stand or fall on such small decisions. A long train of seemingly small abuses can create a large revolution, as we Americans, of all people, should know.

There is another reason, which has been lost in the public debate. Liberal education, an education adequate to serve the life of a free and equal citizen in any modern democracy, requires far more than the reading of great books, although great books are an indispensable aid. We also need to read and think about books, and therefore to teach them, in a spirit of free and open inquiry, the spirit of both democratic citizenship and individual freedom. The cultivation of that spirit is aided by immersion in profound and influential books, like Plato's *Republic*, which expose us to eloquently original, systematically well-reasoned, intimidating, and unfamiliar visions of the good life and good society. But liberal education fails if intimidation leads to blind acceptance of those visions or if unfamiliarity leads us to blind rejection.

These two signs of failure are too often reflected in the public debate over multiculturalism on college and university campuses. In resisting the substitution of new works for old ones, essentialists suggest that the insights and truths of the old will be lost by even partial substitution, which is typically what is at stake in controversies like the one at Stanford. But preservation of tried-and-true verities is not among the best reasons for including the classics in any list of required reading at the university level. Why not say that great books like Plato's *Republic* or Aristotle's *Politics* are among the most challenging to anyone who wants to think carefully, systematically, and critically about politics? It is intellectual idolatry, and not philosophical openness and acuity, that supports the claim, frequently articulated but rarely defended, that the greatest philosophical works—judged by such standards as originality and eloquence, systematic reasoning, depth of moral, psychological, or political understanding, and influence on our inherited social understandings—contain the greatest wisdom now available to us on all significant subjects.

Is Aristotle's understanding of slavery more enlightening than Frederick Douglass's? Is Aquinas's argument about civil disobedience more defensible than Martin Luther King's or John Rawls's? If not, then why not assign students *The Autobiography of Frederick Douglass*, "Letter from Birmingham City Jail," and *A Theory of Justice* alongside the *Politics* and *Summa Theologiae*? Although Rousseau's understanding of women challenges contemporary feminism, it is far less credible or compelling on intellectual grounds than Virginia Woolf's, Simone de Beauvoir's, or Toni Morrison's insights on women. Similarly, Hannah Arendt offers a perspective on political evil that goes beyond that of any canonical political philosopher. Were essentialists explicitly to open their public argument to the possibility that the classics do not contain comprehensive or timeless truths on all significant subjects, they could moderate their critique and recognize the reasonableness of some proposed reforms that create more multicultural curricula.

A significant internal obstacle that stands in the way of moderation is the belief held in reserve by some essentialists that the classics, especially the works of Plato and Aristotle, are the key to timeless moral and political truths, the truths of human nature. In the spirit of Robert Maynard Hutchins, essentialists often invoke Plato, Aristotle, and "nature" as critical standards. The argument, explicitly made by Hutchins but only intimated by Allan Bloom and other contemporary critics, goes roughly as follows: The highest form of human nature is the same in America as in Athens, as should be the content of higher education, if it is to be true to the highest in human nature, the intellectual virtues cultivated to their greatest perfection. Here is Hutchins' succinct formulation: "Education implies teaching. Teaching implies knowledge. Knowledge is truth. The truth is everywhere the same. Hence education should be everywhere the same. I do not overlook the possibilities of differences in organization, in administration, in local habits and customs. These are details."[1] Essentialists honor and invoke the great books as the critical standard for judging both "lesser" works and societies that inevitably fail to live up to Platonic or Aristotelian standards.

One need not in any way denigrate the great books or defend a standardless relativism to worry about the way in which the essentialist critique of multiculturalism partakes of intellectual idol worship. Compare the essentialist defense of the canon to Ralph Waldo Emerson's approach to books, as argued in "The American Scholar." Emerson's perspective serves as an important challenge to essentialism, and yet no contemporary critic takes up this challenge: "The theory of books is noble. . . . But none is quite perfect. As no air-

---

[1] Robert Maynard Hutchins, *The Higher Learning in America* (New Haven: Yale University Press, 1936), p. 66.

pump can by any means make a perfect vacuum, so neither can any artist entirely exclude the conventional, the local, the perishable from his book, or write a book of pure thought, that shall be as efficient, in all respects, to a remote posterity, as to contemporaries, or rather to the second age."[2] Emerson is not saying that because even the best books are to some significant extent conventional and rooted in a particular social context, we should read them primarily for what they reflect about their own times rather than what they can say to us and our times. We can still learn a lot about the human condition from Plato's *Republic*, or about our obligation to the state from the *Crito*. But we cannot learn everything profound about obligation, let alone everything worth knowing about the human condition, from reading Plato, Aristotle, or the entire corpus of canonical works.

"Each age," Emerson concludes, "must write its own books."[3] Why? Because well-educated, open-minded people and liberal democratic citizens must think for themselves. In liberal democracies, a primary aim of liberal arts universities is not to create bookworms, but to cultivate people who are willing and able to be self-governing in both their political and personal lives. "Books are the best of things, well used," Emerson argues, "abused, among the worst. What is the right use? . . . They are for nothing but to inspire."[4]

It would also be a form of intellectual idolatry to take Emerson's words as gospel. Books do more than inspire. They also unite us in a community, or communities, of learning. They teach us about our intellectual heritage, our culture, as well as about foreign cultures. American universities may aspire to be more international, but to the extent that our liberal arts curriculum along with our student body is

[2] Ralph Waldo Emerson, "The American Scholar," in *Selected Essays*, ed. Larzer Ziff (New York: Viking Penguin, 1982), p. 87.
[3] Ibid.
[4] Ibid., p. 88.

still primarily American, it is crucial, as Wolf suggests in her comments, that universities recognize who "we" are when they defend a core curriculum that speaks to "our" circumstances, culture, and intellectual heritage. Not because students can identify only with works written by authors of the same race, ethnicity, or gender, but because there are books by and about women, African-Americans, Asian-Americans, and Native Americans that speak to neglected parts of our heritage and human condition, and speak more wisely than do some of the canonical works. Although social injustices concern us all, neglect of noncanonical literature is more acutely perceived by people who identify themselves with the neglected, and the exclusion of such works is not unreasonably thought to reflect lack of respect for members of these groups, or disregard for part of their cultural identities. Criticism of the canon per se should not therefore be equated with tribalism or particularism. Emerson was guilty of neither when he argued that each age must write, and presumably also read, its own books.

Radically opposed to essentialism, deconstructionists erect a different obstacle to liberal democratic education when they deny the desirability of shared intellectual standards, which scholars and students of diverse cultural backgrounds might use to evaluate our common education. Although deconstructionists do not deny the possibility of shared standards, they view common standards as masks for the will to political power of dominant, hegemonic groups. This reductionist argument about intellectual standards is often made on behalf of groups that are underrepresented in the university and disadvantaged in society, but it is hard to see how it can come to the aid of anyone. The argument is self-undermining, both logically and practically. By its internal logic, deconstructionism has nothing more to say for the view that intellectual standards are masks for the will to political power than that it too reflects the will to power of deconstructionists. But why then bother with intellectual life at all,

18

which is not the fastest, surest, or even most satisfying path to political power, if it is political power that one is really after?

Deconstructionism is also impractical. If intellectual standards are political in the sense of reflecting the antagonistic interests and will to power of particular groups, then disadvantaged groups have no choice but to accept the hegemonic standards that society imposes on the academy and the academy in turn imposes on them. The less powerful cannot possibly hope to have their standards win out, especially if their academic spokespersons publicize the view that intellectual standards are nothing more than assertions or reflections of the will to power.

The deconstructionist outlook on the academy not only deconstructs itself, it does so in a dangerous way. Deconstructionists do not *act* as if they believed that common standards are impossible. They act, and often speak, as if they believed that the university curriculum *should* include works by and about disadvantaged groups. And some version of this position, as we have seen, is defensible on universalistic grounds. But the reduction of all intellectual disagreements to conflicts of group interests is not. It does not stand up to evidence or reasoned argument. Anyone who doubts this conclusion might try to demonstrate in a nontautological way that the *strongest* arguments for and against legalizing abortion, not the arguments offered by politicians but the most careful and compelling philosophical arguments, simply reflect the will to power, class and gender interests of their proponents.

Reductionism of intellect and argument to political interest threatens to politicize the university more profoundly and destructively than ever before. I say "threatens" because deconstructionism has not actually "taken over" the academy, as some critics claim. But the anti-intellectual, politicizing threat it poses is nonetheless real. A great deal of intellectual life, especially in the humanities and the "soft" social sciences, depends upon dialogue among reasonable people who disagree on the answers to some fundamental questions about the value of various literary, political, economic, religious, educational, scientific, and aesthetic understandings and achievements. Colleges and universities are the only major social institutions dedicated to fostering knowledge, understanding, intellectual dialogue, and the pursuit of reasoned argument in the many directions that it may lead. The threat of deconstructionism to intellectual life in the academy is twofold: (1) it denies *a priori* that there are any reasonable answers to fundamental questions, and (2) it reduces every answer to an exercise of political power.

Taken seriously, on its own terms, the deconstructionist defense of a more multicultural curriculum itself appears as an assertion of political power in the name of the exploited and oppressed, rather than as an intellectually defensible reform. And deconstructionism represents critics and criticisms of multiculturalism, however reasonable, as politically retrograde and unworthy of intellectual respect. Whereas essentialists react to reasonable uncertainty and disagreement by invoking rather than defending timeless truths, deconstructionists react by explaining away our different viewpoints, presuming they are equally indefensible on intellectual grounds. Intellectual life is deconstructed into a political battlefield of class, gender, and racial interests, an analogy that does not do justice to democratic politics at its best, which is not merely a contest of competing interest groups. But the image conveyed of academic life, the real arena of deconstructionist activity, is more dangerous still because it can create its own reality, converting universities into political battlefields rather than mutually respectful communities of substantial, sometimes even fundamental, intellectual disagreement.

Deconstructionists and essentialists disagree about the value and content of a multicultural curriculum. The disagreement is exacerbated by the zero-sum nature of the choice between canonical and newer works, when a few required core courses become the focus in academic and public discussions of what constitutes a good education. But disagreement about what books should be required and how they should be read is not in itself terribly troubling. No university curriculum can possibly include all the books or represent all the cultures worthy of recognition in a liberal democratic education. Nor can any free society, let alone any university of independent scholars and teachers, expect to agree on hard choices between competing goods. The cause for concern about the ongoing controversies over multiculturalism and the curriculum is rather that the most vocal parties to these disputes appear unwilling to defend their views before people with whom they disagree, and to entertain seriously the possibility of change in the face of well-reasoned criticism. Instead, in an equal and opposite reaction, essentialists and deconstructionists express mutual disdain rather than respect for their differences. And so they create two mutually exclusive and disrespecting intellectual cultures in academic life, evincing an attitude of unwillingness to learn anything from the other or recognize any value in the other. In political life writ large, there is a parallel problem of disrespect and lack of constructive communication among the spokespersons for ethnic, religious, and racial groups, a problem that all too often leads to violence.

The survival of many mutually exclusive and disrespecting cultures is not the moral promise of multiculturalism, in politics or in education. Nor is it a realistic vision: neither universities nor polities can effectively pursue their valued ends without mutual respect among the various cultures they contain. But not every aspect of cultural diversity is worthy of respect. Some differences—racism and anti-Semitism are obvious examples—ought not to be *respected*, even if expressions of racist and anti-Semitic views must be *tolerated*.

The controversy on college campuses over racist, ethnic, sexist, homophobic, and other forms of offensive speech directed against members of disadvantaged groups exemplifies the need for a shared moral vocabulary that is richer than our rights to free speech. Suppose one grants that members of a university community should have the right to express racist, anti-Semitic, sexist, and homophobic views provided they do not threaten anyone. What is left to say about the racist, anti-Semitic, sexist, and homophobic remarks that have become increasingly common on college campuses? Nothing, if our shared moral vocabulary is limited to the right of free speech, unless one challenges racist and anti-Semitic statements on free speech grounds. But then the public issue will quickly shift from the pernicious content of the speech to the speaker's right of free speech.

Everything is left to say, however, if we can distinguish between tolerating and respecting differences. Toleration extends to the widest range of views, so long as they stop short of threats and other direct and discernible harms to individuals. Respect is far more discriminating. Although we need not agree with a position to respect it, we must understand it as reflecting a moral point of view. Someone with a pro-choice position on abortion, for example, should be able to understand how a morally serious person without ulterior motives might be opposed to legalizing abortion. There are serious moral arguments to be made against legalization. And vice versa. A multicultural society is bound to include a wide range of such respectable moral disagreements, which offers us the opportunity to defend our views before morally serious people with whom we disagree and thereby learn from our differences. In this way, we can make a virtue out of the necessity of our moral disagreements.

There is no virtue in misogyny, racial and ethnic hatred, or rationalizations of self-interest and group interest parading as historical or scientific knowledge. Undeserving of respect are views that flagrantly disregard the interests of others and therefore do not take a genuine moral position at all, or that make radically implausible empirical claims (of racial inferiority, for example) that are not grounded upon publicly shared or accessible standards of evidence. Incidents of hate speech on college campuses fall into this category of disrespectable speech. Racist and anti-Semitic slogans are indefensible on moral and empirical grounds, and add nothing valuable to democratic deliberation or intellectual life. They reflect a refusal to treat people as equals, along with an unwillingness or inability to provide publicly accessible evidence for presuming other groups of people fundamentally inferior to oneself and one's group. Hate speech violates the most elementary moral injunction to respect the dignity of all human beings, and simply *presumes* the fundamental inferiority of others.

As communities dedicated to intellectual inquiry, universities should give the broadest protection to free speech. But, having protected everyone's right to speak, university communities need not and should not be silent when faced with racist, anti-Semitic, or other disrespectable speech. Members of academic communities—faculty, students, and administrators—can use our right to free speech to denounce disrespectable speech by exposing it for what it is, flagrant disregard for the interests of other people, rationalization of self-interest or group interest, prejudice, or sheer hatred of humanity. There is no valuable understanding to be gained directly from the content of disrespectable speech. Even so, incidents of hate speech challenge members of liberal democratic communities to articulate the most fundamental moral presuppositions that unite us. We fail ourselves and, more importantly, the targets of hate speech if we do not respond to the often unthinking, sometimes drunken disregard for the most elementary standards of human decency.

Respectable moral disagreements, on the other hand, call for deliberation, not denunciation. Colleges and universities can serve as models for deliberation, by encouraging rigorous, honest, open, and intense intellectual discussions, both inside and outside the classroom. The willingness and ability to deliberate about our respectable differences is also part of the democratic political ideal. Multicultural societies and communities that stand for the freedom and equality of all people rest upon mutual respect for reasonable intellectual, political, and cultural differences. Mutual respect requires a widespread willingness and ability to articulate our disagreements, to defend them before people with whom we disagree, to discern the difference between respectable and disrespectable disagreement, and to be open to changing our own minds when faced with well-reasoned criticism. The moral promise of multiculturalism depends on the exercise of these deliberative virtues.

The Politics of Recognition

CHARLES TAYLOR

I

A NUMBER of strands in contemporary politics turn on the need, sometimes the demand, for *recognition*. The need, it can be argued, is one of the driving forces behind nationalist movements in politics. And the demand comes to the fore in a number of ways in today's politics, on behalf of minority or "subaltern" groups, in some forms of feminism and in what is today called the politics of "multiculturalism."

The demand for recognition in these latter cases is given urgency by the supposed links between recognition and identity, where this latter term designates something like a person's understanding of who they are, of their fundamental defining characteristics as a human being. The thesis is that our identity is partly shaped by recognition or its absence, often by the *mis*recognition of others, and so a person or group of people can suffer real damage, real distortion, if the people or society around them mirror back to them a confining or demeaning or contemptible picture of themselves. Nonrecognition or misrecognition can inflict harm, can be a form of oppression, imprisoning someone in a false, distorted, and reduced mode of being.

Thus some feminists have argued that women in patriarchal societies have been induced to adopt a depreciatory image of themselves. They have internalized a picture of their own inferiority, so that even when some of the objective obstacles to their advancement fall away, they may be incapable of taking advantage of the new opportunities. And beyond this, they are condemned to suffer the pain of low self-esteem. An analogous point has been made in relation to blacks: that white society has for generations projected a demeaning image of them, which some of them have been unable to resist adopting. Their own self-depreciation, on this view, becomes one of the most potent instruments of their own oppression. Their first task ought to be to purge themselves of this imposed and destructive identity. Recently, a similar point has been made in relation to indigenous and colonized people in general. It is held that since 1492 Europeans have projected an image of such people as somehow inferior, "uncivilized," and through the force of conquest have often been able to impose this image on the conquered. The figure of Caliban has been held to epitomize this crushing portrait of contempt of New World aboriginals.

Within these perspectives, misrecognition shows not just a lack of due respect. It can inflict a grievous wound, saddling its victims with a crippling self-hatred. Due recognition is not just a courtesy we owe people. It is a vital human need.

In order to examine some of the issues that have arisen here, I'd like to take a step back, achieve a little distance, and look first at how this discourse of recognition and identity came to seem familiar, or at least readily understandable, to us. For it was not always so, and our ancestors of more than a couple of centuries ago would have stared at us uncomprehendingly if we had used these terms in their current sense. How did we get started on this?

Hegel comes to mind right off, with his famous dialectic of the master and the slave. This is an important stage, but we need to go a little farther back to see how this passage came to have the sense it did. What changed to make this kind of talk have sense for us?

We can distinguish two changes that together have made the modern preoccupation with identity and recognition inevitable. The first is the collapse of social hierarchies, which used to be the basis for honor. I am using *honor* in the ancien régime sense in which it is intrinsically linked to inequalities. For some to have honor in this sense, it is essential that not everyone have it. This is the sense in which Montesquieu uses it in his description of monarchy. Honor is intrinsically a matter of "préférences."[1] It is also the sense in which we use the term when we speak of honoring someone by giving her some public award, for example, the Order of Canada. Clearly, this award would be without worth if tomorrow we decided to give it to every adult Canadian.

As against this notion of honor, we have the modern notion of dignity, now used in a universalist and egalitarian sense, where we talk of the inherent "dignity of human beings," or of citizen dignity. The underlying premise here is that everyone shares in it.[2] It is obvious that this concept of dignity is the only one compatible with a democratic society, and that it was inevitable that the old concept of honor was superseded. But this has also meant that the forms of equal recognition have been essential to democratic culture. For instance, that everyone be called "Mr.," "Mrs.," or "Miss," rather than some people being called "Lord" or "Lady" and others simply by their surnames—or, even more demeaning, by their first names—has been thought essential in some democratic societies, such as the United States. More recently, for similar reasons, "Mrs." and "Miss" have been collapsed into "Ms." Democracy has ushered in a politics of equal recognition, which has taken various forms over the years, and has now returned in the form of demands for the equal status of cultures and of genders.

---

[1] "La nature de l'honneur est de demander des préférences et des distinctions. . . ." Montesquieu, *De l'esprit des lois*, Bk. 3, chap. 7.

[2] The significance of this move from "honor" to "dignity" is interestingly discussed by Peter Berger in his "On the Obsolescence of the Concept of Honour," in *Revisions: Changing Perspectives in Moral Philosophy*, ed. Stanley Hauerwas and Alasdair MacIntyre (Notre Dame, Ind.: University of Notre Dame Press, 1983), pp. 172–81.

But the importance of recognition has been modified and intensified by the new understanding of individual identity that emerges at the end of the eighteenth century. We might speak of an *individualized* identity, one that is particular to me, and that I discover in myself. This notion arises along with an ideal, that of being true to myself and my own particular way of being. Following Lionel Trilling's usage in his brilliant study, I will speak of this as the ideal of "authenticity."[3] It will help to describe in what it consists and how it came about.

One way of describing its development is to see its starting point in the eighteenth-century notion that human beings are endowed with a moral sense, an intuitive feeling for what is right and wrong. The original point of this doctrine was to combat a rival view, that knowing right and wrong was a matter of calculating consequences, in particular, those concerned with divine reward and punishment. The idea was that understanding right and wrong was not a matter of dry calculation, but was anchored in our feelings.[4] Morality has, in a sense, a voice within.

The notion of authenticity develops out of a displacement of the moral accent in this idea. On the original view, the inner voice was important because it tells us what the right thing to do is. Being in touch with our moral feelings matters here, as a means to the end of acting rightly. What I'm calling the displacement of the moral accent comes about when being in touch with our feelings takes on independent and crucial moral significance. It comes to be something we have to attain if we are to be true and full human beings.

To see what is new here, we have to see the analogy to earlier moral views, where being in touch with some source—for example, God, or the Idea of the Good—was

[3] Lionel Trilling, *Sincerity and Authenticity* (New York: Norton, 1969).

[4] I have discussed the development of this doctrine at greater length, at first in the work of Francis Hutcheson, drawing on the writings of the Earl of Shaftesbury, and its adversarial relation to Locke's theory in *Sources of the Self* (Cambridge, Mass.: Harvard University Press, 1989), chap. 15.

considered essential to full being. But now the source we have to connect with is deep within us. This fact is part of the massive subjective turn of modern culture, a new form of inwardness, in which we come to think of ourselves as beings with inner depths. At first, this idea that the source is within doesn't exclude our being related to God or the Ideas; it can be considered our proper way of relating to them. In a sense, it can be seen as just a continuation and intensification of the development inaugurated by Saint Augustine, who saw the road to God as passing through our own self-awareness. The first variants of this new view were theistic, or at least pantheistic.

The most important philosophical writer who helped to bring about this change was Jean-Jacques Rousseau. I think Rousseau is important not because he inaugurated the change; rather, I would argue that his great popularity comes in part from his articulating something that was in a sense already occurring in the culture. Rousseau frequently presents the issue of morality as that of our following a voice of nature within us. This voice is often drowned out by the passions that are induced by our dependence on others, the main one being *amour propre*, or pride. Our moral salvation comes from recovering authentic moral contact with ourselves. Rousseau even gives a name to the intimate contact with oneself, more fundamental than any moral view, that is a source of such joy and contentment: "le sentiment de l'existence."[5]

---

[5] "Le sentiment de l'existence dépouillé de toute autre affection est par lui-même un sentiment précieux de contentement et de paix qui suffiroit seul pour rendre cette existence chère et douce à qui sauroit écarter de soi toutes les impressions sensuelles et terrestres qui viennent sans cesse nous en distraire et en troubler ici bas la douceur. Mais la pluspart des hommes agités de passions continuelles connoissent peu cet état et ne l'ayant gouté qu'imparfaitement durant peu d'instans n'en conservent qu'une idée obscure et confuse qui ne leur en fait pas sentir le charme." Jean-Jacques Rousseau, *Les Rêveries du promeneur solitaire*, "Cinquième Promenade," in *Oeuvres complètes* (Paris: Gallimard, 1959), 1:1047.

The ideal of authenticity becomes crucial owing to a development that occurs after Rousseau, which I associate with the name of Herder—once again, as its major early articulator, rather than its originator. Herder put forward the idea that each of us has an original way of being human: each person has his or her own "measure."[6] This idea has burrowed very deep into modern consciousness. It is a new idea. Before the late eighteenth century, no one thought that the differences between human beings had this kind of moral significance. There is a certain way of being human that is *my* way. I am called upon to live my life in this way, and not in imitation of anyone else's life. But this notion gives a new importance to being true to myself. If I am not, I miss the point of my life; I miss what being human is for *me*.

This is the powerful moral ideal that has come down to us. It accords moral importance to a kind of contact with myself, with my own inner nature, which it sees as in danger of being lost, partly through the pressures toward outward conformity, but also because in taking an instrumental stance toward myself, I may have lost the capacity to listen to this inner voice. It greatly increases the importance of this self-contact by introducing the principle of originality: each of our voices has something unique to say. Not only should I not mold my life to the demands of external conformity; I can't even find the model by which to live outside myself. I can only find it within.[7]

[6] "Jeder Mensch hat ein eigenes Maass, gleichsam eine eigne Stimmung aller seiner sinnlichen Gefühle zu einander." Johann Gottlob Herder, *Ideen*, chap. 7, sec. 1, in *Herders Sämtliche Werke*, ed. Bernard Suphan (Berlin: Weidmann, 1877–1913), 13:291.

[7] John Stuart Mill was influenced by this Romantic current of thought when he made something like the ideal of authenticity the basis for one of his most powerful arguments in *On Liberty*. See especially chapter 3, where he argues that we need something more than a capacity for "apelike imitation": "A person whose desires and impulses are his own—are the expression of his own nature, as it has been developed and modified by his own culture—is said to have a character." "If a person possesses

Being true to myself means being true to my own original-ity, which is something only I can articulate and discover. In articulating it, I am also defining myself. I am realizing a po-tentiality that is properly my own. This is the background understanding to the modern ideal of authenticity, and to the goals of self-fulfillment and self-realization in which the ideal is usually couched. I should note here that Herder ap-plied his conception of originality at two levels, not only to the individual person among other persons, but also to the culture-bearing people among other peoples. Just like indi-viduals, a *Volk* should be true to itself, that is, its own cul-ture. Germans shouldn't try to be derivative and (inevitably) second-rate Frenchmen, as Frederick the Great's patronage seemed to be encouraging them to do. The Slavic peoples had to find their own path. And European colonialism ought to be rolled back to give the peoples of what we now call the Third World their chance to be themselves unimpeded. We can recognize here the seminal idea of modern nationalism, in both benign and malignant forms.

This new ideal of authenticity was, like the idea of dignity, also in part an offshoot of the decline of hierarchical society. In those earlier societies, what we would now call identity was largely fixed by one's social position. That is, the back-ground that explained what people recognized as important to themselves was to a great extent determined by their place in society, and whatever roles or activities attached to this position. The birth of a democratic society doesn't by itself do away with this phenomenon, because people can still de-fine themselves by their social roles. What does decisively undermine this socially derived identification, however, is the ideal of authenticity itself. As this emerges, for instance,

---

any tolerable amount of common sense and experience, his own mode of laying out his existence is the best, not because it is the best in itself, but because it is his own mode." John Stuart Mill, *Three Essays* (Oxford: Ox-ford University Press, 1975), pp. 73, 74, 83.

31

with Herder, it calls on me to discover my own original way of being. By definition, this way of being cannot be socially derived, but must be inwardly generated.

But in the nature of the case, there is no such thing as inward generation, monologically understood. In order to understand the close connection between identity and recognition, we have to take into account a crucial feature of the human condition that has been rendered almost invisible by the overwhelmingly monological bent of mainstream modern philosophy.

This crucial feature of human life is its fundamentally *dialogical* character. We become full human agents, capable of understanding ourselves, and hence of defining our identity, through our acquisition of rich human languages of expression. For my purposes here, I want to take *language* in a broad sense, covering not only the words we speak, but also other modes of expression whereby we define ourselves, including the "languages" of art, of gesture, of love, and the like. But we learn these modes of expression through exchanges with others. People do not acquire the languages needed for self-definition on their own. Rather, we are introduced to them through interaction with others who matter to us—what George Herbert Mead called "significant others."[8] The genesis of the human mind is in this sense not monological, not something each person accomplishes on his or her own, but dialogical.

Moreover, this is not just a fact about *genesis*, which can be ignored later on. We don't just learn the languages in dialogue and then go on to use them for our own purposes. We are of course expected to develop our own opinions, outlook, stances toward things, and to a considerable degree through solitary reflection. But this is not how things work with important issues, like the definition of our identity. We

[8] George Herbert Mead, *Mind, Self, and Society* (Chicago: University of Chicago Press, 1934).

define our identity always in dialogue with, sometimes in struggle against, the things our significant others want to see in us. Even after we outgrow some of these others—our parents, for instance—and they disappear from our lives, the conversation with them continues within us as long as we live.[9]

Thus, the contribution of significant others, even when it is provided at the beginning of our lives, continues indefinitely. Some people may still want to hold on to some form of the monological ideal. It is true that we can never liberate ourselves completely from those whose love and care shaped us early in life, but we should strive to define ourselves on our own to the fullest extent possible, coming as best we can to understand and thus get some control over the influence of our parents, and avoiding falling into any more such dependent relationships. We need relationships to fulfill, but not to define, ourselves.

The monological ideal seriously underestimates the place of the dialogical in human life. It wants to confine it as much as possible to the genesis. It forgets how our understanding of the good things in life can be transformed by our enjoying them in common with people we love; how some goods become accessible to us only through such common enjoyment. Because of this, it would take a great deal of effort, and probably many wrenching break-ups, to *prevent* our identity's being formed by the people we love. Consider what we mean by *identity*. It is who we are, "where we're coming from." As such it is the background against which our tastes and desires and opinions and aspirations make

[9] This inner dialogicality has been explored by M. M. Bakhtin and those who have drawn on his work. See, of Bakhtin, especially *Problems of Dostoyevsky's Poetics*, trans. Caryl Emerson (Minneapolis: University of Minnesota Press, 1984). See also Michael Holquist and Katerina Clark, *Mikhail Bakhtin* (Cambridge, Mass.: Harvard University Press, 1984); and James Wertsch, *Voices of the Mind* (Cambridge, Mass.: Harvard University Press, 1991).

sense. If some of the things I value most are accessible to me only in relation to the person I love, then she becomes part of my identity.

To some people this might seem a limitation, from which one might aspire to free oneself. This is one way of understanding the impulse behind the life of the hermit or, to take a case more familiar to our culture, the solitary artist. But from another perspective, we might see even these lives as aspiring to a certain kind of dialogicality. In the case of the hermit, the interlocutor is God. In the case of the solitary artist, the work itself is addressed to a future audience, perhaps still to be created by the work. The very form of a work of art shows its character as *addressed*.[10] But however one feels about it, the making and sustaining of our identity, in the absence of a heroic effort to break out of ordinary existence, remains dialogical throughout our lives.

Thus my discovering my own identity doesn't mean that I work it out in isolation, but that I negotiate it through dialogue, partly overt, partly internal, with others. That is why the development of an ideal of inwardly generated identity gives a new importance to recognition. My own identity crucially depends on my dialogical relations with others.

Of course, the point is not that this dependence on others arose with the age of authenticity. A form of dependence was always there. The socially derived identity was by its very nature dependent on society. But in the earlier age recognition never arose as a problem. General recognition was built into the socially derived identity by virtue of the very fact that it was based on social categories that everyone took for granted. Yet inwardly derived, personal, original identity doesn't enjoy this recognition *a priori*. It has to win it through

[10] See Bakhtin, "The Problem of the Text in Linguistics, Philology and the Human Sciences," in *Speech Genres and Other Late Essays*, ed. Caryl Emerson and Michael Holquist (Austin: University of Texas Press, 1986), p. 126, for this notion of a "super-addressee," beyond our existing interlocutors.

exchange, and the attempt can fail. What has come about with the modern age is not the need for recognition but the conditions in which the attempt to be recognized can fail. That is why the need is now acknowledged for the first time. In premodern times, people didn't speak of "identity" and "recognition"—not because people didn't have (what we call) identities, or because these didn't depend on recognition, but rather because these were then too unproblematic to be thematized as such.

It's not surprising that we can find some of the seminal ideas about citizen dignity and universal recognition, even if not in these specific terms, in Rousseau, whom I have wanted to identify as one of the points of origin of the modern discourse of authenticity. Rousseau is a sharp critic of hierarchical honor, of "préférences." In a significant passage of the *Discourse on Inequality*, he pinpoints a fateful moment when society takes a turn toward corruption and injustice, when people begin to desire preferential esteem.[11] By contrast, in republican society, where all can share equally in the light of public attention, he sees the source of health.[12] But

---

[11] Rousseau is describing the first assemblies: "Chacun commença à regarder les autres et à vouloir être regardé soi-même, et l'estime publique eut un prix. Celui qui chantait ou dansait le mieux; le plus beau, le plus fort, le plus adroit ou le plus éloquent devint le plus considéré, et ce fut là le premier pas vers l'inégalité, et vers le vice en même temps." *Discours sur l'origine et les fondements de l'inégalité parmi les hommes* (Paris: Granier-Flammarion, 1971), p. 210.

[12] See, for example, the passage in the *Considérations sur le gouvernement de Pologne* where he describes the ancient public festival, in which all the people took part, in *Du contrat social* (Paris: Garnier, 1962), p. 345; and also the parallel passage in *Lettre à D'Alembert sur les spectacles*, in *Du contrat social*, pp. 224–25. The crucial principle was that there should be no division between performers and spectators, but that all should be seen by all. "Mais quels seront enfin les objets de ces spectacles? Qu'y montrera-t-on? Rien, si l'on veut. . . . Donnez les spectateurs en spectacles; rendez-les acteurs eux-mêmes; faites que chacun se voie et s'aime dans les autres, que tous en soient mieux unis."

the topic of recognition is given its most influential early treatment in Hegel.[13]

The importance of recognition is now universally acknowledged in one form or another; on an intimate plane, we are all aware of how identity can be formed or malformed through the course of our contact with significant others. On the social plane, we have a continuing politics of equal recognition. Both planes have been shaped by the growing ideal of authenticity, and recognition plays an essential role in the culture that has arisen around this ideal.

On the intimate level, we can see how much an original identity needs and is vulnerable to the recognition given or withheld by significant others. It is not surprising that in the culture of authenticity, relationships are seen as the key loci of self-discovery and self-affirmation. Love relationships are not just important because of the general emphasis in modern culture on the fulfillments of ordinary needs. They are also crucial because they are the crucibles of inwardly generated identity.

On the social plane, the understanding that identities are formed in open dialogue, unshaped by a predefined social script, has made the politics of equal recognition more central and stressful. It has, in fact, considerably raised the stakes. Equal recognition is not just the appropriate mode for a healthy democratic society. Its refusal can inflict damage on those who are denied it, according to a widespread modern view, as I indicated at the outset. The projection of an inferior or demeaning image on another can actually distort and oppress, to the extent that the image is internalized. Not only contemporary feminism but also race relations and discussions of multiculturalism are undergirded by the premise that the withholding of recognition can be a form of oppression. We may debate whether this factor has been exagger-

[13] See Hegel, *The Phenomenology of Spirit*, trans. A. V. Miller (Oxford: Oxford University Press, 1977), chap. 4.

ated, but it is clear that the understanding of identity and authenticity has introduced a new dimension into the politics of equal recognition, which now operates with something like its own notion of authenticity, at least so far as the denunciation of other-induced distortions is concerned.

II

And so the discourse of recognition has become familiar to us, on two levels: First, in the intimate sphere, where we understand the formation of identity and the self as taking place in a continuing dialogue and struggle with significant others. And then in the public sphere, where a politics of equal recognition has come to play a bigger and bigger role. Certain feminist theories have tried to show the links between the two spheres.[14]

I want to concentrate here on the public sphere, and try to work out what a politics of equal recognition has meant and could mean.

In fact, it has come to mean two rather different things, connected, respectively, with the two major changes I have been describing. With the move from honor to dignity has come a politics of universalism, emphasizing the equal dignity of all citizens, and the content of this politics has been the equalization of rights and entitlements. What is to be avoided at all costs is the existence of "first-class" and "second-class" citizens. Naturally, the actual detailed measures justified by this principle have varied greatly, and have often

---

[14] There are a number of strands that have linked these two levels, but perhaps special prominence in recent years has been given to a psychoanalytically oriented feminism, which roots social inequalities in the early upbringing of men and women. See, for instance, Nancy Chodorow, *Feminism and Psychoanalytic Theory* (New Haven: Yale University Press, 1989); and Jessica Benjamin, *Bonds of Love: Psychoanalysis, Feminism and the Problem of Domination* (New York: Pantheon, 1988).

been controversial. For some, equalization has affected only civil rights and voting rights; for others, it has extended into the socioeconomic sphere. People who are systematically handicapped by poverty from making the most of their citizenship rights are deemed on this view to have been relegated to second-class status, necessitating remedial action through equalization. But through all the differences of interpretation, the principle of equal citizenship has come to be universally accepted. Every position, no matter how reactionary, is now defended under the colors of this principle. Its greatest, most recent victory was won by the civil rights movement of the 1960s in the United States. It is worth noting that even the adversaries of extending voting rights to blacks in the southern states found some pretext consistent with universalism, such as "tests" to be administered to would-be voters at the time of registration.

By contrast, the second change, the development of the modern notion of identity, has given rise to a politics of difference. There is, of course, a universalist basis to this as well, making for the overlap and confusion between the two. *Everyone* should be recognized for his or her unique identity. But recognition here means something else. With the politics of equal dignity, what is established is meant to be universally the same, an identical basket of rights and immunities; with the politics of difference, what we are asked to recognize is the unique identity of this individual or group, their distinctness from everyone else. The idea is that it is precisely this distinctness that has been ignored, glossed over, assimilated to a dominant or majority identity. And this assimilation is the cardinal sin against the ideal of authenticity.[15]

---

[15] A prime example of this charge from a feminist perspective is Carol Gilligan's critique of Lawrence Kohlberg's theory of moral development, for presenting a view of human development that privileges only one facet of moral reasoning, precisely the one that tends to predominate in boys rather than girls. See Gilligan, *In a Different Voice* (Cambridge, Mass.: Harvard University Press, 1982).

Now underlying the demand is a principle of universal equality. The politics of difference is full of denunciations of discrimination and refusals of second-class citizenship. This gives the principle of universal equality a point of entry within the politics of dignity. But once inside, as it were, its demands are hard to assimilate to that politics. For it asks that we give acknowledgment and status to something that is not universally shared. Or, otherwise put, we give due acknowledgment only to what is universally present—everyone has an identity—through recognizing what is peculiar to each. The universal demand powers an acknowledgment of specificity.

The politics of difference grows organically out of the politics of universal dignity through one of those shifts with which we are long familiar, where a new understanding of the human social condition imparts a radically new meaning to an old principle. Just as a view of human beings as conditioned by their socioeconomic plight changed the understanding of second-class citizenship, so that this category came to include, for example, people in inherited poverty traps, so here the understanding of identity as formed in interchange, and as possibly so malformed, introduces a new form of second-class status into our purview. As in the present case, the socioeconomic redefinition justified social programs that were highly controversial. For those who had not gone along with this changed definition of equal status, the various redistributive programs and special opportunities offered to certain populations seemed a form of undue favoritism.

Similar conflicts arise today around the politics of difference. Where the politics of universal dignity fought for forms of nondiscrimination that were quite "blind" to the ways in which citizens differ, the politics of difference often redefines nondiscrimination as requiring that we make these distinctions the basis of differential treatment. So members of aboriginal bands will get certain rights and powers not enjoyed by other Canadians, if the demands for native self-government are finally agreed on, and certain minorities will get the right to exclude others in order to preserve their cultural integrity, and so on.

To proponents of the original politics of dignity, this can seem like a reversal, a betrayal, a simple negation of their cherished principle. Attempts are therefore made to mediate, to show how some of these measures meant to accommodate minorities can after all be justified on the original basis of dignity. These arguments can be successful up to a point. For instance, some of the (apparently) most flagrant departures from "difference-blindness" are reverse discrimination measures, affording people from previously unfavored groups a competitive advantage for jobs or places in universities. This practice has been justified on the grounds that historical discrimination has created a pattern within which the unfavored struggle at a disadvantage. Reverse discrimination is defended as a temporary measure that will eventually level the playing field and allow the old "blind" rules to come back into force in a way that doesn't disadvantage anyone. This argument seems cogent enough—wherever its factual basis is sound. But it won't justify some of the measures now urged on the grounds of difference, the goal of which is not to bring us back to an eventual "difference-blind" social space but, on the contrary, to maintain and cherish distinctness, not just now but forever. After all, if we're concerned with identity, then what is more legitimate than one's aspiration that it never be lost?[16]

[16] Will Kymlicka, in his very interesting and tightly argued book *Liberalism, Community and Culture* (Oxford: Clarendon Press, 1989), tries to argue for a kind of politics of difference, notably in relation to aboriginal rights in Canada, but from a basis that is firmly within a theory of liberal neutrality. He wants to argue on the basis of certain cultural needs—minimally, the need for an integral and undamaged cultural language with which one can define and pursue his or her own conception of the good life. In certain circumstances, with disadvantaged populations, the integrity of the

So even though one politics springs from the other, by one of those shifts in the definition of key terms with which we're familiar, the two diverge quite seriously from each other. One basis for the divergence comes out even more clearly when we go beyond what each requires that we acknowledge—certain universal rights in one case, a particular identity on the other—and look at the underlying intuitions of value.

The politics of equal dignity is based on the idea that all humans are equally worthy of respect. It is underpinned by a notion of what in human beings commands respect, however we may try to shy away from this "metaphysical" background. For Kant, whose use of the term *dignity* was one of the earliest influential evocations of this idea, what commanded respect in us was our status as rational agents, capable of directing our lives through principles.[17] Something like this has been the basis for our intuitions of equal dignity ever since, though the detailed definition of it may have changed.

Thus, what is picked out as of worth here is a *universal human potential*, a capacity that all humans share. This potential, rather than anything a person may have made of it, is what ensures that each person deserves respect. Indeed, our sense of the importance of potentiality reaches so far that we

---

culture may require that we accord them more resources or rights than others. The argument is quite parallel to that made in relation to socio-economic inequalities that I mentioned above.

But where Kymlicka's interesting argument fails to recapture the actual demands made by the groups concerned—say Indian bands in Canada, or French-speaking Canadians—is with respect to their goal of survival. Kymlicka's reasoning is valid (perhaps) for *existing* people who find themselves trapped within a culture under pressure, and can flourish within it or not at all. But it doesn't justify measures designed to ensure survival through indefinite future generations. For the populations concerned, however, that is what is at stake. We need only think of the historical resonance of "la survivance" among French Canadians.

[17] See Kant, *Grundlegung der Metaphysik der Sitten* (Berlin: Gruyter, 1968; reprint of the Berlin Academy edition), p. 434.

extend this protection even to people who through some circumstance that has befallen them are incapable of realizing their potential in the normal way—handicapped people, or those in a coma, for instance.

In the case of the politics of difference, we might also say that a universal potential is at its basis, namely, the potential for forming and defining one's own identity, as an individual, and also as a culture. This potentiality must be respected equally in everyone. But at least in the intercultural context, a stronger demand has recently arisen: that one accord equal respect to actually evolved cultures. Critiques of European or white domination, to the effect that they have not only suppressed but failed to appreciate other cultures, consider these depreciatory judgments not only factually mistaken but somehow morally wrong. When Saul Bellow is famously quoted as saying something like, "When the Zulus produce a Tolstoy we will read him,"[18] this is taken as a quintessential statement of European arrogance, not just because Bellow is allegedly being *de facto* insensitive to the value of Zulu culture, but frequently also because it is seen to reflect a denial in principle of human equality. The possibility that the Zulus, while having the same potential for culture formation as anyone else, might nevertheless have come up with a culture that is less valuable than others is ruled out from the start. Even to entertain this possibility is to deny human equality. Bellow's error here, then, would not be a (possibly insensitive) particular mistake in evaluation, but a denial of a fundamental principle.

To the extent that this stronger reproach is in play, the demand for equal recognition extends beyond an acknowledgment of the equal value of all humans potentially, and comes to include the equal value of what they have made of this

---

[18] I have no idea whether this statement was actually made in this form by Saul Bellow, or by anyone else. I report it only because it captures a widespread attitude, which is, of course, why the story had currency in the first place.

potential in fact. This creates a serious problem, as we shall see below.

These two modes of politics, then, both based on the notion of equal respect, come into conflict. For one, the principle of equal respect requires that we treat people in a difference-blind fashion. The fundamental intuition that humans command this respect focuses on what is the same in all. For the other, we have to recognize and even foster particularity. The reproach the first makes to the second is just that it violates the principle of nondiscrimination. The reproach the second makes to the first is that it negates identity by forcing people into a homogeneous mold that is untrue to them. This would be bad enough if the mold were itself neutral— nobody's mold in particular. But the complaint generally goes further. The claim is that the supposedly neutral set of difference-blind principles of the politics of equal dignity is in fact a reflection of one hegemonic culture. As it turns out, then, only the minority or suppressed cultures are being forced to take alien form. Consequently, the supposedly fair and difference-blind society is not only inhuman (because suppressing identities) but also, in a subtle and unconscious way, itself highly discriminatory.[19]

This last attack is the cruelest and most upsetting of all. The liberalism of equal dignity seems to have to assume that there are some universal, difference-blind principles. Even though we may not have defined them yet, the project of

[19] One hears both kinds of reproach today. In the context of some modes of feminism and multiculturalism, the claim is the strong one, that the hegemonic culture discriminates. In the Soviet Union, however, alongside a similar reproach leveled at the hegemonic Great Russian culture, one also hears the complaint that Marxist-Leninist communism has been an alien imposition on all equally, even on Russia itself. The communist mold, on this view, has been truly nobody's. Solzhenitsyn has made this claim, but it is voiced by Russians of a great many different persuasions today, and has something to do with the extraordinary phenomenon of an empire that has broken apart through the quasi-secession of its metropolitan society.

defining them remains alive and essential. Different theories may be put forward and contested—and a number have been proposed in our day[20]—but the shared assumption of the different theories is that one such theory is right.

The charge leveled by the most radical forms of the politics of difference is that "blind" liberalisms are themselves the reflection of particular cultures. And the worrying thought is that this bias might not just be a contingent weakness of all hitherto proposed theories, that the very idea of such a liberalism may be a kind of pragmatic contradiction, a particularism masquerading as the universal.

I want now to try to move, gently and gingerly, into this nest of issues, glancing at some of the important stages in the emergence of these two kinds of politics in Western societies. I will first look at the politics of equal dignity.

III

The politics of equal dignity has emerged in Western civilization in two ways, which we could associate with the names of two standard-bearers, Rousseau and Kant. This doesn't mean that all instances of each have been influenced by these masters (though that is arguably true for the Rousseauean branch), just that Rousseau and Kant are prominent early exponents of the two models. Looking at the two models should enable us to gauge to what extent they are guilty of the charge of imposing a false homogeneity.

I stated earlier, at the end of the first section, that I thought that Rousseau could be seen as one of the originators of the discourse of recognition. I say this not because he

[20] See John Rawls, *A Theory of Justice* (Cambridge, Mass.: Harvard University Press, 1971); Ronald Dworkin, *Taking Rights Seriously* (London: Duckworth, 1977) and *A Matter of Principle* (Cambridge, Mass.: Harvard University Press, 1985); and Jürgen Habermas, *Theorie des kommunikativen Handelns* (Frankfurt: Suhrkamp, 1981).

uses the term, but because he begins to think out the importance of equal respect, and, indeed, deems it indispensable for freedom. Rousseau, as is well known, tends to oppose a condition of freedom-in-equality to one characterized by hierarchy and other-dependence. In this state, one is dependent on others not just because they wield political power, or because one needs them for survival or success in one's cherished projects, but above all because one craves their esteem. The other-dependent person is a slave to "opinion."

This idea is one of the keys to the connection that Rousseau assumes between other-dependence and hierarchy. Logically, these two things would seem separable. Why can't there be other-dependence in conditions of equality? It seems that for Rousseau this cannot be, because he associates other-dependence with the need for others' good opinion, which in turn is understood in the framework of the traditional conception of honor, that is, as intrinsically bound up with "préférences." The esteem we seek in this condition is intrinsically differential. It is a positional good.

It is because of this crucial place of honor within it that the depraved condition of mankind has a paradoxical combination of properties such that we are unequal in power, and yet *all* dependent on others—not just the slave on the master, but also the master on the slave. This point is frequently made. The second sentence of *The Social Contract*, after the famous first line about men being born free and yet being everywhere in chains, runs: "Tel se croit le maître des autres, qui ne laisse pas d'être plus esclave qu'eux [One thinks himself the master of others, and still remains a greater slave than they]."[21] And in *Emile* Rousseau tells us that in this condition of dependence, "maître et esclave se dépravent mutuellement [master and slave corrupt each other]."[22] If

---

[21] *The Social Contract and Discourses*, trans. G.D.H. Cole (New York: E. P. Dutton, 1950), pp. 3–4.

[22] *Emile* (Paris: Garnier, 1964), Bk. 2, p. 70.

it were simply a question of brute power, one might think the master free at the expense of the slave. But in a system of hierarchical honor, the deference of the lower orders is essential.

Rousseau often sounds like the Stoics, who undoubtedly influenced him. He identifies pride (*amour propre*) as one of the great sources of evil. But he doesn't end up where the Stoics do. There is a long-standing discourse on pride, both Stoic and Christian, that recommends that we completely overcome our concern for the good opinion of others. We are asked to step outside this dimension of human life, in which reputations are sought, gained, and unmade. How you appear in public space should be of no concern to you. Rousseau sometimes sounds as if he is endorsing this line. In particular, it is part of his own self-dramatization that he could maintain his integrity in the face of undeserved hostility and calumny from the world. But when we look at his accounts of a potentially good society, we can see that esteem does still play a role in them, that people live very much in the public gaze. In a functioning republic, the citizens do care very much what others think. In a passage of the *Considerations on the Government of Poland*, Rousseau describes how ancient legislators took care to attach citizens to their fatherland. One of the means used to achieve this connection was public games. Rousseau speaks of the prizes with which,

> aux acclamations de toute la Grèce, on couronnoit les vainqueurs dans leurs jeux qui, les embrasant continuellement d'émulation et de gloire, portèrent leur courage et leurs vertus à ce degré d'énergie dont rien aujourd'hui ne nous donne l'idée, et qu'il n'appartient pas même aux modernes de croire.

> [Successful contestants in Greek games were crowned amidst applause from all their fellow-citizens—these are the things that, by constantly re-kindling the spirit of emulation and the love of glory, raised Greek courage and Greek virtues to a level of strenuousness of which nothing existing today can

give us even a remote idea—which, indeed, strikes modern men as beyond belief.][23]

Glory, public recognition, mattered very much here. Moreover, the effect of their mattering was highly beneficent. Why is this so, if modern honor is such a negative force?

The answer seems to be equality, or, more exactly, the balanced reciprocity that underpins equality. One might say (though Rousseau didn't) that in these ideal republican contexts, everyone did depend on everyone else, but all did so equally. Rousseau is arguing that the key feature of these events, games, festivals, and recitations, which made them sources of patriotism and virtue, was the total lack of differentiation or distinction between different classes of citizen. They took place in the open air, and they involved everyone. People were both spectator and show. The contrast drawn in this passage is with modern religious services in enclosed churches, and above all with modern theater, which operates in closed halls, which you have to pay to get into, and consists of a special class of professionals making presentations to others.

This theme is central to the *Letter to D'Alembert*, where again Rousseau contrasts modern theater and the public festivals of a true republic. The latter take place in the open air. Here he makes it clear that the identity of spectator and performer is the key to these virtuous assemblies.

> Mais quels seront les objets de ces spectacles? Qu'y montrera-t-on? Rien, si l'on veut. Avec la liberté, partout où régne l'affluence, le bien-être y régne aussi. Plantez au milieu d'une place un piquet couronné de fleurs, rassemblez-y le peuple, et vous aurez une fête. Faîtes mieux encore: donnez les spectateurs en spectacle; rendez-les acteurs eux-mêmes; faîtes que

---

[23] *Considerations sur le gouvernement de Pologne*, p. 345; *Considerations on the Government of Poland*, trans. Wilmoore Kendall (Indianapolis: Bobbs-Merrill, 1972), p. 8.

chacun se voie et s'aime dans les autres, afin que tous en soient mieux unis.

[But what then will be the objects of these entertainments? What will be shown in them? Nothing, if you please. With liberty, wherever abundance reigns, well-being also reigns. Plant a stake crowned with flowers in the middle of a square; gather the people together there, and you will have a festival. Do better yet; let the spectators become an entertainment to themselves; make them actors themselves; do it so that each sees and loves himself in the others so that all will be better united.][24]

Rousseau's underlying, unstated argument would seem to be this: A perfectly balanced reciprocity takes the sting out of our dependence on opinion, and makes it compatible with liberty. Complete reciprocity, along with the unity of purpose that it makes possible, ensures that in following opinion I am not in any way pulled outside myself. I am still "obeying myself" as a member of this common project or "general will." Caring about esteem in this context is compatible with freedom and social unity, because the society is one in which all the virtuous will be esteemed equally and for the same (right) reasons. In contrast, in a system of hierarchical honor, we are in competition; one person's glory must be another's shame, or at least obscurity. Our unity of purpose is shattered, and in this context attempting to win the favor of another, who by hypothesis has goals distinct from mine, must be alienating. Paradoxically, the bad other-dependence goes along with separation and isolation;[25] the

[24] *Lettre à D'Alembert*, p. 225; *Letter to M. D'Alembert on the Theatre*, in Jean-Jacques Rousseau, *Politics and the Arts*, trans. Allan Bloom (Ithaca, N.Y.: Cornell University Press, 1968), p. 126.

[25] A little later in the passage I quoted above from the *Considerations on the Government of Poland*, Rousseau describes gatherings in our depraved modern society as "des cohues licencieuses," where people go "pour s'y faire des liaisons secrètes, pour y chercher les plaisirs qui séparent, isolent

good kind, which Rousseau doesn't call other-dependence at all, involves the unity of a common project, even a "common self."[26]

Thus Rousseau is at the origin of a new discourse about honor and dignity. To the two traditional ways of thinking about honor and pride he adds a third, which is quite different. There was a discourse denouncing pride, as I mentioned above, which called on us to remove ourselves from this whole dimension of human life and to be utterly unconcerned with esteem. And then there was an ethic of honor, frankly nonuniversalist and inegalitarian, which saw the concern with honor as the first mark of the honorable man. Someone unconcerned with reputation, unwilling to defend it, had to be a coward, and therefore contemptible.

Rousseau borrows the denunciatory language of the first discourse, but he doesn't end up calling for a renunciation of all concern with esteem. On the contrary, in his portrait of the republican model, caring about esteem is central. What is wrong with pride or honor is its striving after preferences, hence division, hence real other-dependence, and therefore loss of the voice of nature, and consequently corruption, the forgetting of boundaries, and effeminacy. The remedy is not rejecting the importance of esteem, but entering into a quite different system, characterized by equality, reciprocity, and unity of purpose. This unity makes possible the equality of esteem, but the fact that esteem is in principle equal in this system is essential to this unity of purpose itself. Under the aegis of the general will, all virtuous citizens are to be equally honored. The age of dignity is born.

---

le plus les hommes, et qui relâchent le plus les coeurs." *Considerations sur le gouvernement de Pologne*, p. 346.

[26] *Du contrat social*, p. 244. I have benefited, in this area, from discussions with Natalie Oman. See her "Forms of Common Space in the Work of Jean-Jacques Rousseau" (Master's research paper, McGill University, July 1991).

This new critique of pride, leading not to solitary mortification but to a politics of equal dignity, is what Hegel took up and made famous in his dialectic of the master and the slave. Against the old discourse on the evil of pride, he takes it as fundamental that we can flourish only to the extent that we are recognized. Each consciousness seeks recognition in another, and this is not a sign of a lack of virtue. But the ordinary conception of honor as hierarchical is crucially flawed. It is flawed because it cannot answer the need that sends people after recognition in the first place. Those who fail to win out in the honor stakes remain unrecognized. But even those who do win are more subtly frustrated, because they win recognition from the losers, whose acknowledgment is, by hypothesis, not really valuable, since they are no longer free, self-supporting subjects on the same level with the winners. The struggle for recognition can find only one satisfactory solution, and that is a regime of reciprocal recognition among equals. Hegel follows Rousseau in finding this regime in a society with a common purpose, one in which there is a "'we' that is an 'I', and an 'I' that is a 'we'."[27]

But if we think of Rousseau as inaugurating the new politics of equal dignity, we can argue that his solution is crucially flawed. In terms of the question posed at the beginning of this section, equality of esteem requires a tight unity of purpose that seems to be incompatible with any differentiation. The key to a free polity for Rousseau seems to be a rigorous exclusion of any differentiation of roles. Rousseau's principle seems to be that for any two-place relation R involving power, the condition of a free society is that the two terms joined by the relation be identical. $x R y$ is compatible with a free society only when $x = y$. This is true when the relation involves the x's presenting themselves in public space to the y's, and it is of course famously true when the

[27] Hegel, *Phenomenology of Spirit*, p. 110.

relation is "exercises sovereignty over." In the social contract state, the people must be both sovereign and subject.

In Rousseau, three things seem to be inseparable: freedom (nondomination), the absence of differentiated roles, and a very tight common purpose. We must all be dependent on the general will, lest there arise bilateral forms of dependence.[28] This has been the formula for the most terrible forms of homogenizing tyranny, starting with the Jacobins and extending to the totalitarian regimes of our century. But even where the third element of the trinity is set aside, the aligning of equal freedom with the absence of differentiation has remained a tempting mode of thought. Wherever it reigns, be it in modes of feminist thought or of liberal politics, the margin to recognize difference is very small.

IV

We might well agree with the above analysis, and want to get some distance from the Rousseauean model of citizen dignity. Yet still we might want to know whether any politics of equal dignity, based on the recognition of universal capacities, is bound to be equally homogenizing. Is this true of those models—which I inscribed above, perhaps rather arbitrarily, under the banner of Kant—that separate equal freedom from both other elements of the Rousseauean trinity? These models not only have nothing to do with a general will, but abstract from any issue of the differentiation of roles. They simply look to an equality of rights accorded to citizens. Yet this form of liberalism has come under attack by radical proponents of the politics of difference as in some

---

[28] In justifying his famous (or infamous) slogan about the person coerced to obey the law being "forced to be free," Rousseau goes on: "car telle est la condition qui donnant chaque citoyen à la Patrie le garantit de toute dépendance personnelle. . . ." *Du contrat social*, p. 246.

way unable to give due acknowledgment to distinctness. Are the critics correct?

The fact is that there are forms of this liberalism of equal rights that in the minds of their own proponents can give only a very restricted acknowledgment of distinct cultural identities. The notion that any of the standard schedules of rights might apply differently in one cultural context than they do in another, that their application might have to take account of different collective goals, is considered quite unacceptable. The issue, then, is whether this restrictive view of equal rights is the only possible interpretation. If it is, then it would seem that the accusation of homogenization is well founded. But perhaps it is not. I think it is not, and perhaps the best way to lay out the issue is to see it in the context of the Canadian case, where this question has played a role in the impending breakup of the country. In fact, two conceptions of rights-liberalism have confronted each other, albeit in confused fashion, throughout the long and inconclusive constitutional debates of recent years.

The issue came to the fore because of the adoption in 1982 of the Canadian Charter of Rights, which aligned our political system in this regard with the American one in having a schedule of rights offering a basis for judicial review of legislation at all levels of government. The question had to arise how to relate this schedule to the claims for distinctness put forward by French Canadians, and particularly Quebeckers, on the one hand, and aboriginal peoples on the other. Here what was at stake was the desire of these peoples for survival, and their consequent demand for certain forms of autonomy in their self-government, as well as the ability to adopt certain kinds of legislation deemed necessary for survival.

For instance, Quebec has passed a number of laws in the field of language. One regulates who can send their children to English-language schools (not francophones or immigrants); another requires that businesses with more than

52

fifty employees be run in French; a third outlaws commercial signage in any language other than French. In other words, restrictions have been placed on Quebeckers by their government, in the name of their collective goal of survival, which in other Canadian communities might easily be disallowed by virtue of the Charter.[29] The fundamental question was: Is this variation acceptable or not?

The issue was finally raised by a proposed constitutional amendment, named after the site of the conference where it was first drafted, Meech Lake. The Meech amendment proposed to recognize Quebec as a "distinct society," and wanted to make this recognition one of the bases for judicial interpretation of the rest of the constitution, including the Charter. This seemed to open up the possibility for variation in its interpretation in different parts of the country. For many, such variation was fundamentally unacceptable. Examining why brings us to the heart of the question of how rights-liberalism is related to diversity.

The Canadian Charter follows the trend of the last half of the twentieth century, and gives a basis for judicial review on two basic scores. First, it defines a set of individual rights that are very similar to those protected in other charters and bills of rights in Western democracies, for example, in the United States and Europe. Second, it guarantees equal treat-

[29] The Supreme Court of Canada did strike down one of these provisions, the one forbidding commercial signage in languages other than French. But in their judgment the justices agreed that it would have been quite reasonable to demand that all signs be in French, even though accompanied by another language. In other words, it was permissible in their view for Quebec to outlaw unilingual English signs. The need to protect and promote the French language in the Quebec context would have justified it. Presumably this would mean that legislative restrictions on the language of signs in another province might well be struck down for some quite other reason.

Incidentally, the signage provisions are still in force in Quebec, because of a provision of the Charter that in certain cases allows legislatures to override judgments of the courts for a restricted period.

ment of citizens in a variety of respects, or, alternatively put, it protects against discriminatory treatment on a number of irrelevant grounds, such as race or sex. There is a lot more in our Charter, including provisions for linguistic rights and aboriginal rights, that could be understood as according powers to collectivities, but the two themes I singled out dominate in the public consciousness.

This is no accident. These two kinds of provisions are now quite common in entrenched schedules of rights that provide the basis for judicial review. In this sense, the Western world, perhaps the world as a whole, is following American precedent. The Americans were the first to write out and entrench a bill of rights, which they did during the ratification of their Constitution and as a condition of its successful outcome. One might argue that they weren't entirely clear on judicial review as a method of securing those rights, but this rapidly became the practice. The first amendments protected individuals, and sometimes state governments,[30] against encroachment by the new federal government. It was after the Civil War, in the period of triumphant Reconstruction, and particularly with the Fourteenth Amendment, which called for "equal protection" for all citizens under the laws, that the theme of nondiscrimination became central to judicial review. But this theme is now on a par with the older norm of the defense of individual rights, and in public consciousness perhaps even ahead.

For a number of people in "English Canada," a political

---

[30] For instance, the First Amendment, which forbade Congress to establish any religion, was not originally meant to separate church and state as such. It was enacted at a time when many states had established churches, and it was plainly meant to prevent the new federal government from interfering with or overruling these local arrangements. It was only later, after the Fourteenth Amendment, following the so-called Incorporation doctrine, that these restrictions on the federal government were held to have been extended to all governments, at any level.

society's espousing certain collective goals threatens to run against both of these basic provisions of our Charter, or indeed any acceptable bill of rights. First, the collective goals may require restrictions on the behavior of individuals that may violate their rights. For many nonfrancophone Canadians, both inside and outside Quebec, this feared outcome had already materialized with Quebec's language legislation. For instance, Quebec legislation prescribes, as already mentioned, the type of school to which parents can send their children; and in the most famous instance, it forbids certain kinds of commercial signage. This latter provision was actually struck down by the Supreme Court as contrary to the Quebec Bill of Rights, as well as the Charter, and only reenacted through the invocation of a clause in the Charter that permits legislatures in certain cases to override decisions of the courts relative to the Charter for a limited period of time (the so-called notwithstanding clause).

But second, even if overriding individual rights were not possible, espousing collective goals on behalf of a national group can be thought to be inherently discriminatory. In the modern world it will always be the case that not all those living as citizens under a certain jurisdiction will belong to the national group thus favored. This in itself could be thought to provoke discrimination. But beyond this, the pursuit of the collective end will probably involve treating insiders and outsiders differently. Thus the schooling provisions of Law 101 forbid (roughly speaking) francophones and immigrants to send their children to English-language schools, but allow Canadian anglophones to do so.

This sense that the Charter clashes with basic Quebec policy was one of the grounds of opposition in the rest of Canada to the Meech Lake accord. The cause for concern was the distinct society clause, and the common demand for amendment was that the Charter be "protected" against this clause, or take precedence over it. There was undoubtedly in this opposition a certain amount of old-style anti-Quebec prejudice, but there was also a serious philosophical point, which we need to articulate here.

Those who take the view that individual rights must always come first, and, along with nondiscrimination provisions, must take precedence over collective goals, are often speaking from a liberal perspective that has become more and more widespread in the Anglo-American world. Its source is, of course, the United States, and it has recently been elaborated and defended by some of the best philosophical and legal minds in that society, including John Rawls, Ronald Dworkin, Bruce Ackerman, and others.[31] There are various formulations of the main idea, but perhaps the one that encapsulates most clearly the point that is relevant to us is the one expressed by Dworkin in his short paper entitled "Liberalism."[32]

Dworkin makes a distinction between two kinds of moral commitment. We all have views about the ends of life, about what constitutes a good life, which we and others ought to strive for. But we also acknowledge a commitment to deal fairly and equally with each other, regardless of how we conceive our ends. We might call this latter commitment "procedural," while commitments concerning the ends of life are "substantive." Dworkin claims that a liberal society is one that as a society adopts no particular substantive view about the ends of life. The society is, rather, united around a strong procedural commitment to treat people with equal respect. The reason that the polity as such can espouse no substan

[31] Rawls, *A Theory of Justice* and "Justice as Fairness: Political Not Metaphysical," *Philosophy & Public Affairs* 14 (1985): 223–51; Dworkin, *Taking Rights Seriously* and "Liberalism," in *Public and Private Morality*, ed. Stuart Hampshire (Cambridge: Cambridge University Press, 1978); Bruce Ackerman, *Social Justice in the Liberal State* (New Haven: Yale University Press, 1980).

[32] Dworkin, "Liberalism."

tive view, cannot, for instance, allow that one of the goals of legislation should be to make people virtuous in one or another meaning of that term, is that this would involve a violation of its procedural norm. For, given the diversity of modern societies, it would unfailingly be the case that some people and not others would be commited to the favored conception of virtue. They might be in a majority; indeed, it is very likely that they would be, for otherwise a democratic society probably would not espouse their view. Nevertheless, this view would not be everyone's view, and in espousing this substantive outlook the society would not be treating the dissident minority with equal respect. It would be saying to them, in effect, "your view is not as valuable, in the eyes of this polity, as that of your more numerous compatriots."

There are very profound philosophical assumptions underlying this view of liberalism, which is rooted in the thought of Immanuel Kant. Among other features, this view understands human dignity to consist largely in autonomy, that is, in the ability of each person to determine for himself or herself a view of the good life. Dignity is associated less with any particular understanding of the good life, such that someone's departure from this would detract from his or her own dignity, than with the power to consider and espouse for oneself some view or other. We are not respecting this power equally in all subjects, it is claimed, if we raise the outcome of some people's deliberations officially over that of others. A liberal society must remain neutral on the good life, and restrict itself to ensuring that however they see things, citizens deal fairly with each other and the state deals equally with all.

The popularity of this view of the human agent as primarily a subject of self-determining or self-expressive choice helps to explain why this model of liberalism is so strong. But we must also consider that it has been urged with great force and intelligence by liberal thinkers in the United States, and precisely in the context of constitutional doctrines of judicial review.[33] Thus it is not surprising that the idea has become widespread, well beyond those who might subscribe to a specific Kantian philosophy, that a liberal society cannot accommodate publicly espoused notions of the good. This is the conception, as Michael Sandel has noted, of the "procedural republic," which has a very strong hold on the political agenda in the United States, and which has helped to place increasing emphasis on judicial review on the basis of constitutional texts at the expense of the ordinary political process of building majorities with a view to legislative action.[34]

But a society with collective goals like Quebec's violates this model. It is axiomatic for Quebec governments that the survival and flourishing of French culture in Quebec is a good. Political society is not neutral between those who value remaining true to the culture of our ancestors and those who might want to cut loose in the name of some individual goal of self-development. It might be argued that one could after all capture a goal like *survivance* for a proceduralist liberal society. One could consider the French language, for instance, as a collective resource that individuals might want to make use of, and act for its preservation, just as one does for clean air or green spaces. But this can't capture the full thrust of policies designed for cultural survival. It is not just a matter of having the French language available for those who might choose it. This might be seen to be the goal of some of the measures of federal bilingualism over the last twenty years. But it also involves making sure that there is a community of people here in the future that will want to avail itself of the opportunity to use the French language. Policies aimed at survival actively seek to *create* members of

[33] See, for instance, the arguments deployed by Lawrence Tribe in his *Abortion: The Clash of Absolutes* (New York: Norton, 1990).

[34] Michael Sandel, "The Procedural Republic and the Unencumbered Self," *Political Theory* 12 (1984): 81–96.

the community, for instance, in their assuring that future generations continue to identify as French-speakers. There is no way that these policies could be seen as just providing a facility to already existing people.

Quebeckers, therefore, and those who give similar importance to this kind of collective goal, tend to opt for a rather different model of a liberal society. On their view, a society can be organized around a definition of the good life, without this being seen as a depreciation of those who do not personally share this definition. Where the nature of the good requires that it be sought in common, this is the reason for its being a matter of public policy. According to this conception, a liberal society singles itself out as such by the way in which it treats minorities, including those who do not share public definitions of the good, and above all by the rights it accords to all of its members. But now the rights in question are conceived to be the fundamental and crucial ones that have been recognized as such from the very beginning of the liberal tradition: rights to life, liberty, due process, free speech, free pracice of religion, and so on. On this model, there is a dangerous overlooking of an essential boundary in speaking of fundamental rights to things like commercial signage in the language of one's choice. One has to distinguish the fundamental liberties, those that should never be infringed and therefore ought to be unassailably entrenched, on one hand, from privileges and immunities that are important, but that can be revoked or restricted for reasons of public policy—although one would need a strong reason to do this—on the other.

A society with strong collective goals can be liberal, on this view, provided it is also capable of respecting diversity, especially when dealing with those who do not share its common goals; and provided it can offer adequate safeguards for fundamental rights. There will undoubtedly be tensions and difficulties in pursuing these objectives together, but such a pursuit is not impossible, and the problems are not in principle greater than those encountered by any liberal society that has to combine, for example, liberty and equality, or prosperity and justice.

Here are two incompatible views of liberal society. One of the great sources of our present disharmony is that the two views have squared off against each other in the last decade. The resistance to the "distinct society" that called for precedence to be given to the Charter came in part from a spreading procedural outlook in English Canada. From this point of view, attributing the goal of promoting Quebec's distinct society to a government is to acknowledge a collective goal, and this move had to be neutralized by being subordinated to the existing Charter. From the standpoint of Quebec, this attempt to impose a procedural model of liberalism not only would deprive the distinct society clause of some of its force as a rule of interpretation, but bespoke a rejection of the model of liberalism on which this society was founded. Each society misperceived the other throughout the Meech Lake debate. But here both perceived each other accurately—and didn't like what they saw. The rest of Canada saw that the distinct society clause legitimated collective goals. And Quebec saw that the move to give the Charter precedence imposed a form of liberal society that was alien to it, and to which Quebec could never accommodate itself without surrendering its identity.[35]

I have delved deeply into this case because it seems to me to illustrate the fundamental questions. There is a form of the politics of equal respect, as enshrined in a liberalism of rights, that is inhospitable to difference, because (a) it insists on uniform application of the rules defining these rights, without exception, and (b) it is suspicious of collective goals. Of course, this doesn't mean that this model seeks to abolish cultural differences. This would be an absurd accusation. But

[35] See Guy Laforest, "L'esprit de 1982," in *Le Québec et la restructuration du Canada, 1980–1992*, ed. Louis Balthasar, Guy Laforest, and Vincent Lemieux (Quebec: Septentrion, 1991).

I call it inhospitable to difference because it can't accommodate what the members of distinct societies really aspire to, which is survival. This is (b) a collective goal, which (a) almost inevitably will call for some variations in the kinds of law we deem permissible from one cultural context to another, as the Quebec case clearly shows.

I think this form of liberalism is guilty as charged by the proponents of a politics of difference. Fortunately, however, there are other models of liberal society that take a different line on (a) and (b). These forms do call for the invariant defense of *certain* rights, of course. There would be no question of cultural differences determining the application of *habeas corpus*, for example. But they distinguish these fundamental rights from the broad range of immunities and presumptions of uniform treatment that have sprung up in modern cultures of judicial review. They are willing to weigh the importance of certain forms of uniform treatment against the importance of cultural survival, and opt sometimes in favor of the latter. They are thus in the end not procedural models of liberalism, but are grounded very much on judgments about what makes a good life—judgments in which the integrity of cultures has an important place.

Although I cannot argue it here, obviously I would endorse this kind of model. Indisputably, though, more and more societies today are turning out to be multicultural, in the sense of including more than one cultural community that wants to survive. The rigidities of procedural liberalism may rapidly become impractical in tomorrow's world.

V

The politics of equal respect, then, at least in this more hospitable variant, can be cleared of the charge of homogenizing difference. But there is another way of formulating the charge that is harder to rebut. In this form, however, it perhaps ought not to be rebutted, or so I want to argue.

The charge I'm thinking of here is provoked by the claim sometimes made on behalf of "difference-blind" liberalism that it can offer a neutral ground on which people of all cultures can meet and coexist. On this view, it is necessary to make a certain number of distinctions—between what is public and what is private, for instance, or between politics and religion—and only then can one relegate the contentious differences to a sphere that does not impinge on the political.

But a controversy like that over Salman Rushdie's *Satanic Verses* shows how wrong this view is. For mainstream Islam, there is no question of separating politics and religion the way we have come to expect in Western liberal society. Liberalism is not a possible meeting ground for all cultures, but is the political expression of one range of cultures, and quite incompatible with other ranges. Moreover, as many Muslims are well aware, Western liberalism is not so much an expression of the secular, postreligious outlook that happens to be popular among liberal *intellectuals* as a more organic outgrowth of Christianity—at least as seen from the alternative vantage point of Islam. The division of church and state goes back to the earliest days of Christian civilization. The early forms of the separation were very different from ours, but the basis was laid for modern developments. The very term *secular* was originally part of the Christian vocabulary.[36]

All this is to say that liberalism can't and shouldn't claim complete cultural neutrality. Liberalism is also a fighting creed. The hospitable variant I espouse, as well as the most rigid forms, has to draw the line. There will be variations when it comes to applying the schedule of rights, but not where incitement to assassination is concerned. But this should not be seen as a contradiction. Substantive distinctions of this kind are inescapable in politics, and at least the

[36] The point is well argued in Larry Siedentop, "Liberalism: The Christian Connection," *Times Literary Supplement*, 24–30 March 1989, p. 308. I have also discussed these issues in "The Rushdie Controversy," in *Public Culture* 2, no. 1 (Fall 1989): 118–22.

nonprocedural liberalism I was describing is fully ready to accept this.

But the controversy is nevertheless disturbing. It is so for the reason I mentioned above: that all societies are becoming increasingly multicultural, while at the same time becoming more porous. Indeed, these two developments go together. Their porousness means that they are more open to multinational migration; more of their members live the life of diaspora, whose center is elsewhere. In these circumstances, there is something awkward about replying simply, "This is how we do things here." This reply must be made in cases like the Rushdie controversy, where "how we do things" covers issues such as the right to life and to freedom of speech. The awkwardness arises from the fact that there are substantial numbers of people who are citizens and also belong to the culture that calls into question our philosophical boundaries. The challenge is to deal with their sense of marginalization without compromising our basic political principles.

This brings us to the issue of multiculturalism as it is often debated today, which has a lot to do with the imposition of some cultures on others, and with the assumed superiority that powers this imposition. Western liberal societies are thought to be supremely guilty in this regard, partly because of their colonial past, and partly because of their marginalization of segments of their populations that stem from other cultures. It is in this context that the reply "this is how we do things here" can seem crude and insensitive. Even if, in the nature of things, compromise is close to impossible here—one either forbids murder or allows it—the attitude presumed by the reply is seen as one of contempt. Often, in fact, this presumption is correct. Thus we arrive again at the issue of recognition.

Recognition of equal value was not what was at stake—at least in a strong sense—in the preceding section. There it was a question of whether cultural survival will be acknowledged as a legitimate goal, whether collective ends will be allowed as legitimate considerations in judicial review, or for other purposes of major social policy. The demand there was that we let cultures defend themselves, within reasonable bounds. But the further demand we are looking at here is that we all *recognize* the equal value of different cultures; that we not only let them survive, but acknowledge their *worth*.

What sense can be made of this demand? In a way, it has been operative in an unformulated state for some time. The politics of nationalism has been powered for well over a century in part by the sense that people have had of being despised or respected by others around them. Multinational societies can break up, in large part because of a lack of (perceived) recognition of the equal worth of one group by another. This is at present, I believe, the case in Canada—though my diagnosis will certainly be challenged by some. On the international scene, the tremendous sensitivity of certain supposedly closed societies to world opinion—as shown in their reactions to findings of, say, Amnesty International, or in their attempts through UNESCO to build a new world information order—attests to the importance of external recognition.

But all this is still *an sich*, not *für sich*, to use Hegelian jargon. The actors themselves are often the first to deny that they are moved by such considerations, and plead other factors, like inequality, exploitation, and injustice, as their motives. Very few Quebec independentists, for instance, can accept that what is mainly winning them their fight is a lack of recognition on the part of English Canada.

What is new, therefore, is that the demand for recognition is now explicit. And it has been made explicit, in the way I indicated above, by the spread of the idea that we are formed by recognition. We could say that, thanks to this idea, misrecognition has now graduated to the rank of a harm that can be hardheadedly enumerated along with the ones mentioned in the previous paragraph.

One of the key authors in this transition is undoubtedly the late Frantz Fanon, whose influential *Les Damnés de la Terre* (*The Wretched of the Earth*)[37] argued that the major weapon of the colonizers was the imposition of their image of the colonized on the subjugated people. These latter, in order to be free, must first of all purge themselves of these depreciating self-images. Fanon recommended violence as the way to this freedom, matching the original violence of the alien imposition. Not all those who have drawn from Fanon have followed him in this, but the notion that there is a struggle for a changed self-image, which takes place both within the subjugated and against the dominator, has been very widely applied. The idea has become crucial to certain strands of feminism, and is also a very important element in the contemporary debate about multiculturalism.

The main locus of this debate is the world of education in a broad sense. One important focus is university humanities departments, where demands are made to alter, enlarge, or scrap the "canon" of accredited authors on the grounds that the one presently favored consists almost entirely of "dead white males." A greater place ought to be made for women, and for people of non-European races and cultures. A second focus is the secondary schools, where an attempt is being made, for instance, to develop Afrocentric curricula for pupils in mainly black schools.

The reason for these proposed changes is not, or not mainly, that all students may be missing something important through the exclusion of a certain gender or certain races or cultures, but rather that women and students from the excluded groups are given, either directly or by omission, a demeaning picture of themselves, as though all creativity and worth inhered in males of European provenance. Enlarging and changing the curriculum is therefore essential not so much in the name of a broader culture for everyone as in

[37] (Paris: Maspero, 1961).

order to give due recognition to the hitherto excluded. The background premise of these demands is that recognition forges identity, particularly in its Fanonist application: dominant groups tend to entrench their hegemony by inculcating an image of inferiority in the subjugated. The struggle for freedom and equality must therefore pass through a revision of these images. Multicultural curricula are meant to help in this process of revision.

Although it is not often stated clearly, the logic behind some of these demands seems to depend upon a premise that we owe equal respect to all cultures. This emerges from the nature of the reproach made to the designers of traditional curricula. The claim is that the judgments of worth on which these latter were supposedly based were in fact corrupt, were marred by narrowness or insensitivity or, even worse, a desire to downgrade the excluded. The implication seems to be that absent these distorting factors, true judgments of value of different works would place all cultures more or less on the same footing. Of course, the attack could come from a more radical, neo-Nietzschean standpoint, which questions the very status of judgments of worth as such, but short of this extreme step (whose coherence I doubt), the presumption seems to be of equal worth.

I would like to maintain that there is something valid in this presumption, but that the presumption is by no means unproblematic, and involves something like an act of faith. As a presumption, the claim is that all human cultures that have animated whole societies over some considerable stretch of time have something important to say to all human beings. I have worded it in this way to exclude partial cultural milieux within a society, as well as short phases of a major culture. There is no reason to believe that, for instance, the different art forms of a given culture should all be of equal, or even of considerable, value; and every culture can go through phases of decadence.

But when I call this claim a "presumption," I mean that it is a starting hypothesis with which we ought to approach the study of any other culture. The validity of the claim has to be demonstrated concretely in the actual study of the culture. Indeed, for a culture sufficiently different from our own, we may have only the foggiest idea *ex ante* of in what its valuable contribution might consist. Because, for a sufficiently different culture, the very understanding of what it is to be of worth will be strange and unfamiliar to us. To approach, say, a raga with the presumptions of value implicit in the well-tempered clavier would be forever to miss the point. What has to happen is what Gadamer has called a "fusion of horizons."[38] We learn to move in a broader horizon, within which what we have formerly taken for granted as the background to valuation can be situated as one possibility alongside the different background of the formerly unfamiliar culture. The "fusion of horizons" operates through our developing new vocabularies of comparison, by means of which we can articulate these contrasts.[39] So that if and when we ultimately find substantive support for our initial presumption, it is on the basis of an understanding of what constitutes worth that we couldn't possibly have had at the beginning. We have reached the judgment partly through transforming our standards.

We might want to argue that we owe all cultures a presumption of this kind. I will explain later on what I think this claim might be based. From this point of view, withholding the presumption might be seen as the fruit merely of prejudice or of ill-will. It might even be tantamount to a denial of equal status. Something like this might lie behind the accusation leveled by supporters of multiculturalism against defenders of the traditional canon. Supposing that their reluctance to enlarge the canon comes from a mixture of prejudice

[38] *Wahrheit und Methode* (Tübingen: Mohr, 1975), pp. 289–90.

[39] I have discussed what is involved here at greater length in "Comparison, History, Truth," in *Myth and Philosophy*, ed. Frank Reynolds and David Tracy (Albany: State University of New York Press, 1990); and in "Understanding and Ethnocentricity," in *Philosophy and the Human Sciences* (Cambridge: Cambridge University Press, 1985).

and ill-will, the multiculturalists charge them with the arrogance of assuming their own superiority over formerly subject peoples.

This presumption would help explain why the demands of multiculturalism build on the already established principles of the politics of equal respect. If withholding the presumption is tantamount to a denial of equality, and if important consequences flow for people's identity from the absence of recognition, then a case can be made for insisting on the universalization of the presumption as a logical extension of the politics of dignity. Just as all must have equal civil rights, and equal voting rights, regardless of race or culture, so all should enjoy the presumption that their traditional culture has value. This extension, however logically it may seem to flow from the accepted norms of equal dignity, fits uneasily within them, as described in Section II, because it challenges the "difference-blindness" that was central to them. Yet it does indeed seem to flow from them, albeit uneasily.

I am not sure about the validity of demanding this presumption as a right. But we can leave this issue aside, because the demand made seems to be much stronger. The claim seems to be that a proper respect for equality requires more than a presumption that further study will make us see things this way, but actual judgments of equal worth applied to the customs and creations of these different cultures. Such judgments seem to be implicit in the demand that certain works be included in the canon, and in the implication that these works have not been included earlier only because of prejudice or ill-will or the desire to dominate. (Of course, the demand for inclusion is *logically* separable from a claim of equal worth. The demand could be: Include these because they're ours, even though they may well be inferior. But this is not how the people making the demand talk.)

But there is something very wrong with the demand in this form. It makes sense to demand as a matter of right that we approach the study of certain cultures with a presumption of their value, as described above. But it can't make sense to demand as a matter of right that we come up with a final concluding judgment that their value is great, or equal to others'. That is, if the judgment of value is to register something independent of our own wills and desires, it cannot be dictated by a principle of ethics. On examination, either we will find something of great value in culture C, or we will not. But it makes no more sense to demand that we do so than it does to demand that we find the earth round or flat, the temperature of the air hot or cold.

I have stated this rather flatly, when as everyone knows there is a vigorous controversy over the "objectivity" of judgments in this field, and whether there is a "truth of the matter" here, as there seems to be in natural science, or indeed, whether even in natural science "objectivity" is a mirage. I do not have space to address this here. I have discussed it somewhat elsewhere.[40] I don't have much sympathy for these forms of subjectivism, which I think are shot through with confusion. But there seems to be some special confusion in invoking them in this context. The moral and political thrust of the complaint concerns unjustified judgments of inferior status allegedly made of nonhegemonic cultures. But if those judgments are ultimately a question of the human will, then the issue of justification falls away. One doesn't, properly speaking, make judgments that can be right or wrong; one expresses liking or dislike, one endorses or rejects another culture. But then the complaint must shift to address the refusal to endorse, and the validity or invalidity of judgments here has nothing to do with it.

Then, however, the act of declaring another culture's creations to be of worth and the act of declaring oneself on their side, even if their creations aren't all that impressive, become indistinguishable. The difference is only in the packaging. Yet the first is normally understood as a genuine expression

[40] See part 1 of *Sources of the Self.*

of respect, the second often as unsufferable patronizing. The supposed beneficiaries of the politics of recognition, the people who might actually benefit from acknowledgment, make a crucial distinction between the two acts. They know that they want respect, not condescension. Any theory that wipes out the distinction seems at least *prima facie* to be distorting crucial facets of the reality it purports to deal with.

In fact, subjectivist, half-baked neo-Nietzschean theories are quite often invoked in this debate. Deriving frequently from Foucault or Derrida, they claim that all judgments of worth are based on standards that are ultimately imposed by and further entrench structures of power. It should be clear why these theories proliferate here. A favorable judgment on demand is nonsense, unless some such theories are valid. Moreover, the giving of such a judgment on demand is an act of breathtaking condescension. No one can really mean it as a genuine act of respect. It is more in the nature of a pretend act of respect given on the insistence of its supposed beneficiary. Objectively, such an act involves contempt for the latter's intelligence. To be an object of such an act of respect demeans. The proponents of neo-Nietzschean theories hope to escape this whole nexus of hypocrisy by turning the entire issue into one of power and counterpower. Then the question is no more one of respect, but of taking sides, of solidarity. But this is hardly a satisfactory solution, because in taking sides they miss the driving force of this kind of politics, which is precisely the search for recognition and respect.

Moreover, even if one could demand it of them, the last thing one wants at this stage from Eurocentered intellectuals is positive judgments of the worth of cultures that they have not intensively studied. For real judgments of worth suppose a fused horizon of standards, as we have seen; they suppose that we have been transformed by the study of the other, so that we are not simply judging by our original familiar standards. A favorable judgment made prematurely

70

would be not only condescending but ethnocentric. It would praise the other for being like us.

Here is another severe problem with much of the politics of multiculturalism. The peremptory demand for favorable judgments of worth is paradoxically—perhaps one should say tragically—homogenizing. For it implies that we already have the standards to make such judgments. The standards we have, however, are those of North Atlantic civilization. And so the judgments implicitly and unconsciously will cram the others into our categories. For instance, we will think of their "artists" as creating "works," which we then can include in our canon. By implicitly invoking our standards to judge all civilizations and cultures, the politics of difference can end up making everyone the same.[41]

In this form, the demand for equal recognition is unacceptable. But the story doesn't simply end there. The enemies of multiculturalism in the American academy have perceived this weakness, and have used this as an excuse to turn their backs on the problem. But this won't do. A response like that attributed to Bellow which I quoted above, to the effect that we will be glad to read the Zulu Tolstoy when he comes along, shows the depths of ethnocentricity. First, there is the implicit assumption that excellence has to take forms familiar to us: the Zulus should produce a *Tolstoy*. Second, we are assuming that their contribution is yet to be made (*when* the Zulus produce a Tolstoy . . .). These two assumptions obvi-

---

[41] The same homogenizing assumptions underlie the negative reaction that many people have to claims to superiority in some definite respect on behalf of Western civilization, say in regard to natural science. But it is absurd to cavil at such claims in principle. If all cultures have made a contribution of worth, it cannot be that these are identical, or even embody the same kind of worth. To expect this would be to vastly underestimate the differences. In the end, the presumption of worth imagines a universe in which different cultures complement each other with quite different kinds of contribution. This picture not only is compatible with, but demands judgments of, superiority-in-a-certain-respect.

ously go hand in hand. If they have to produce our kind of excellence, then obviously their only hope lies in the future. Roger Kimball puts it more crudely: "The multiculturalists notwithstanding, the choice facing us today is not between a 'repressive' Western culture and a multicultural paradise, but between culture and barbarism. Civilization is not a gift, it is an achievement—a fragile achievement that needs constantly to be shored up and defended from besiegers inside and out."[42]

There must be something midway between the inauthentic and homogenizing demand for recognition of equal worth, on the one hand, and the self-immurement within ethnocentric standards, on the other. There are other cultures, and we have to live together more and more, both on a world scale and commingled in each individual society.

What there is is the presumption of equal worth I described above: a stance we take in embarking on the study of the other. Perhaps we don't need to ask whether it's something that others can demand from us as a right. We might simply ask whether this is the way we ought to approach others.

Well, is it? How can this presumption be grounded? One ground that has been proposed is a religious one. Herder, for instance, had a view of divine providence, according to which all this variety of culture was not a mere accident but was meant to bring about a greater harmony. I can't rule out such a view. But merely on the human level, one could argue that it is reasonable to suppose that cultures that have provided the horizon of meaning for large numbers of human beings, of diverse characters and temperaments, over a long period of time—that have, in other words, articulated their sense of the good, the holy, the admirable—are almost certain to have something that deserves our admiration and respect, even if it is accompanied by much that we have to

---

[42] "Tenured Radicals," *New Criterion*, January 1991, p. 13.

abhor and reject. Perhaps one could put it another way: it would take a supreme arrogance to discount this possibility *a priori*.

There is perhaps after all a moral issue here. We only need a sense of our own limited part in the whole human story to accept the presumption. It is only arrogance, or some analogous moral failing, that can deprive us of this. But what the presumption requires of us is not peremptory and inauthentic judgments of equal value, but a willingness to be open to comparative cultural study of the kind that must displace our horizons in the resulting fusions. What it requires above all is an admission that we are very far away from that ultimate horizon from which the relative worth of different cultures might be evident. This would mean breaking with an illusion that still holds many "multiculturalists"—as well as their most bitter opponents—in its grip.[43]

[43] There is a very interesting critique of both extreme camps, from which I have borrowed in this discussion, in Benjamin Lee, "Towards a Critical Internationalism" (forthcoming).

❖

Comment

SUSAN WOLF

Of the many issues Charles Taylor's extraordinarily rich and stimulating essay raises, I have chosen to focus on the one he discusses last, and to explore, as Taylor does, the ways in which the politics of recognition properly bears on the issue of multicultural education. Before turning to this topic, though, I feel a need to remark on one of the paths not taken—namely, one that would have focused on specifically feminist concerns. Professor Taylor rightly notes the common historical and theoretical roots of the demand for recognition and of an appreciation of its importance that are evident in feminist as well as multicultural politics. But there are differences also, both in the harms suffered and in the ways to correct them. It would be a shame if, while acknowledging the importance of recognition, and specifically, the importance of recognizing difference, we failed to recognize the differences among different failures of recognition and among the harms that ensue from them.

The failures of recognition on which Professor Taylor primarily focuses are, first, a failure literally to recognize that the members of one or another minority or underprivileged group *have* a cultural identity with a distinctive set of traditions and practices and a distinctive intellectual and aesthetic history, and, second, a failure to recognize that this cultural identity is of deep importance and value. The harms most obvious in this context are, at the least, that the members of the unrecognized cultures will feel deracinated and empty, lacking the sources for a feeling of community and a basis for

75

self-esteem, and, at the worst, that they will be threatened with the risk of cultural annihilation. The most obvious remedies involve publicizing, admiring, and explicitly preserving the cultural traditions and achievements of these groups, understood as traditions and achievements specifically belonging to the descendants of the relevant cultures.

The situation of women, however, is not fully parallel with that of members of unappreciated cultures. While the predominant demand for recognition in multicultural contexts is the demand to have one's culture and one's cultural identity recognized as such, to have one's identity *as* an African-American or Asian-American or Native American appreciated and respected, the question of whether and how significantly and with what meaning one wants to be recognized as a woman is itself a matter of deep contention. For clearly there is a sense in which women have been recognized as women—indeed, as "nothing but women"—for all too long, and the question of how to move beyond that specific, distorting type of recognition is problematic in part because there is not a clear, or a clearly desirable, separate cultural heritage by which to redefine and reinterpret what it is to have an identity as a woman.

Unlike the French Canadians, or perhaps to a lesser degree the Mormons, the Amish, or the Orthodox Jews living in the United States, women as a group are not remotely threatened with the risk of annihilation as a distinctly gendered group. Despite advances in biotechnology that make the option biologically possible, this particular harm is not one about which women need to worry. The predominant problem for women as women is not that the larger or more powerful sector of the community fails to notice or be interested in preserving women's gendered identity, but that this identity is put to the service of oppression and exploitation. The failures of recognition most evident in this context are, first, a failure to recognize women as individuals, with minds, interests, and talents of their own, who may be more or less uncomfortable with or indifferent to the roles their gender has assigned them, and, second, the failure to recognize the values and the skills involved in the activities traditionally associated with women and the ways in which experience with and attention to those activities may enhance rather than limit one's intellectual, artistic, and professional abilities in other contexts.

One essay could not possibly attend to all of the issues that may fairly be raised under the title "the politics of recognition." Indeed, it is remarkable how much historical, intellectual, and political complexity Taylor has conveyed in so short a space. Still, we may hope that in the long run a more detailed attention to the differences between the most evident problems of recognition for women and the most evident problems of recognition for cultures, as well as attention to the differences within these categories that vary with class, race, religion, and more singular empirical facts, will be able mutually to inform both the theoretical and the practical conclusions we draw when we consider any one of these problems. The problems of women who have been constrained by their role as women can remind us that, say, African-Americans can also be constrained by an intolerant insistence that they give cultural identity a central place in their lives. And the problems of those who have been urged to ignore or suppress or remove their differences from white, Christian heterosexuals can remind us of the dangers of trying to deny the significance of, say, gender differences that may run very deep.

In any event, reflection on one set of problems may shape our perspective when we turn to another set. And it may well be that my recent occupation with issues of gender helps to explain my perspective on the subject to which I now turn.

Specifically, I want to consider, as Taylor has, the demand for the recognition of the diversity of cultures, and particularly the way this demand is expressing itself in the sphere of education. As Professor Taylor notes, the demand for equal respect for different cultures, or for members of and descendants of different cultures, has led to the demand that the contributions of these cultures be recognized—and recognized immediately—as equally valid and valuable. As Taylor also notes, this is a demand that, at least in its most frequent formulations, is internally inconsistent and so impossible to satisfy. For the demand that all cultures and the works they produce be evaluated as equally good is intertwined with a repudiation of all possible standards for evaluation, which would undermine the validity of judgments of equal worth as much as it undermines judgments of inferior worth. Taylor argues, rightly, I think, that the subjectivist strand in these arguments is ultimately destructive to the goals that the arguments are constructed to support. He argues rightly that, although subjectivism offers a quick and easy response to the demands for justifying a revision of the canon, it is a response that ultimately ends in contempt for the very practice of justification, for the vocabulary of critical appreciation, and for anything that could serve as a basis for authentic respect. Thus, he argues (rightly again) that it is a mistake to demand that works of every culture be evaluated, prior to inspection and appreciation, as equally good works, which equally display human accomplishment, and which make equal contributions to the world's store of beauty and brilliance.

Still, I find something oddly disturbing in Taylor's own view about what follows from this, and in his own proposal about what, if we are not to be subjectivists, we must understand the right to recognition legitimately to entail. Taylor suggests that recognition requires us to give all cultures the *presumption* that "[since they] have animated whole societies over some considerable stretch of time [they] have something important to say to all human beings." This would commit us to studying these cultures, to expanding our imaginations and opening our minds so as to put ourselves in a position to see what, if anything, is distinctively valuable in them. In time, when the presumption has paid off, we can shift our justification to one of equal or distinctive worth, for then and only then will we be in a position to understand and articulate what specific and distinctive values each culture has to offer.

It seems to me that this line of thought takes us in an unfortunate direction, that it leads us away from one of the crucial issues that the politics of recognition urges us to address. For at least one of the serious harms that a failure of recognition perpetuates has little to do with the question of whether the person or the culture who goes unrecognized has anything important to say to all human beings. The need to correct those harms, therefore, does not depend on the presumption or the confirmation of the presumption that a particular culture is distinctively valuable to people outside the culture.

One way to bring out what I have in mind is by imagining, unrealistic as it may be, that the hypothetical Saul Bellow actually listens to Taylor and takes his remarks to heart. Presumably, when Bellow allegedly made that remark about Tolstoy and the Zulus, his underlying thought was that the canon that included Tolstoy and all those other dead white males simply represented the best of what world culture has to offer, the masterpieces of human civilization. Now it is pointed out to him that he is not in a position to make that claim—for he is barely acquainted with the achievements of Asian and African and nonwhite American civilization, and even insofar as he is acquainted with them, he is quite incompetent to assess them.

Were Bellow to accept the charge against him, he would thereby acknowledge that his remark had revealed an arrogance of enormous proportions, and that it reflected an outrageous failure of recognition. For in unthinkingly identifying the masterpieces of European culture with the masterpieces of human civilization, he was failing to recognize—

failing even to see—all the human civilization that was not European.

We are to imagine that Bellow does accept the charge, that he now amends his understanding of the canon as representing, not the great works of civilization, but the great works of European civilization. What effect would this have? My own guess is that Bellow, or, if not Bellow, many of his colleagues, would cede the point without altering his views about what the curriculum should be. I imagine him replying, "Well, perhaps I was out of line in describing the canon as representing the achievements of the world. But if it doesn't represent the achievements of the world, at least it represents the achievements of *our* world, of *our* culture, and that's sufficient to justify it as the centerpiece of *our* curriculum."

But this response reveals a second failure of recognition, at least as intolerable as the first. For we must imagine Bellow to be addressing these remarks, at the very least, to his colleagues and students at the University of Chicago. And, elite as that institution is, we know that the group includes many who are not Europeans. He says, referring to white, European culture, "This is our culture." But the audience is not all white, and is not all descended from Europeans. What does he make of all those other bodies in the room?

It is not clear—perhaps it is not determinate—whether the sort of failure of recognition depicted here is better interpreted as a literal exclusion of African-Americans and others from the audience, as if to say, "When I speak of *our* culture, of course, I don't mean *yours*," or whether we should see it as a patronizing willingness to accept those outlying members of the University of Chicago community as honorary whites, honorary Europeans (and probably honorary males). Either way, this sort of failure of recognition is extremely pervasive in our educational institutions, and it constitutes a level of insult and damage in need of immediate remedy.

The insult portrayed here is an insult fundamentally to individuals and not to cultures. It consists either in ignoring the presence of these individuals in our community or in neglecting or belittling the importance of their cultural identities. Failing to respect the existence or importance of their distinctive histories, arts, and traditions, we fail to respect them as equals, whose interests and values have equal standing in our community.

This failure of respect, however, does not depend on any beliefs about the relative merit of one culture compared to another. Nor does the need to remedy it rest on the claim, presumed or confirmed, that African or Asian or Native American culture has anything particularly important to teach the world. It rests on the claim that African and Asian and Native American cultures are part of our culture, or rather, of the cultures of some of the groups that together constitute our community.

Every time I go to the library with my children, I am presented with an illustration of how generations past have failed to recognize the degree to which our community is multicultural, and of how the politics of recognition can lead, and indeed is leading, to a kind of social progress. My children tend to gravitate toward the section with folk stories and fairy tales. They love many of the same stories that I loved as a child—Rapunzel, the Frog Prince, the Musicians of Bremen—but their favorites also include tales from Africa, Asia, Eastern Europe, and Latin America that were unavailable to me when I was growing up.

Did my mother fail to recognize these books as ones I might enjoy? Did she push them back into the stacks, almost as a reflex, when she saw the illustrators' foreign styles or the slanted eyes or dark skin of the characters? Probably she would have, had these books been in the library. But before my mother's powers of recognition could be put to the test, I suspect that others had limited the selection. For the librarians had probably failed to recognize those books as they went through long lists and catalogues, deciding what to order. And the catalogues themselves probably reflected the decisions of editors and publishers who at an earlier stage had failed to recognize, in the manuscripts that were sent to them and in the authors they chose to cultivate and encourage, the potential to interest, please, and more generally reward that the retelling of these stories possessed.

Remarkable progress has been made in this area, I think, with remarkable results. Obviously, one important result is that African-American children, Asian-American children, and others can find books in the library expressing and illustrating traditions and legends to which they are more closely tied and books in which the characters look and speak more like they and their parents and grandparents do. Another is that people with stories to tell and pictures to paint that express the traditions and the life of these cultures recognize that they have these things to offer and that there is an audience to receive them joyfully. Yet another is that *all* American children now have available to them a diversity of literary and artistic styles—and, simply, a diversity of stories—that could constitute the beginning of a truly multicultural heritage. When one child with this exposure encounters another, she neither expects him to be the same as she nor sees him as alien or foreign.

In fact, the storybooks and legends from these other lands and other cultures are as rewarding to me and my children as the German and French fairy tales with which the children's libraries of my generation were filled—they provide as much delight to the ear and the eye, and inspire the imagination as fully. But the value I want to emphasize in applauding this multicultural expansion of available folktales is not directly or primarily related to a comparative assessment of these stories' literary value. The most significant harm to which the previous failures of recognition in our libraries contributed was not that we were deprived access to some

great folktales, as great as or even greater than the ones represented on the shelves. For there never was a shortage of
great stories for children to read or a competition to determine which single story was the very best. The most significant good, or at least the one I wish to emphasize, is not that
our stock of legends is now better or more comprehensive
than before. It is, rather, that by having these books and by
reading them, we come to recognize ourselves as a multicultural community and so to recognize and respect the members of that community in all our diversity.

How these considerations bear on the subject of university
education—and, even more specifically, on the subject of revising the canon—is a complex matter, for the goals of a university education, the appropriate methods for achieving
these goals, the responsibilities of public as opposed to private institutions, are all matters of controversy in relation to
which discussions of the value of multiculturalism must be
placed. Surely, one goal of university education is to ac-
quaint students with and teach students how to appreciate
great literature, *great* art, *great* philosophy, and the *best* of
scientific theory and method. With respect to this goal, the
judgment that one artwork or idea or theory is objectively
better than another, insofar as such judgments can intelli-
gibly and sensibly be made, will be relevant to curriculum
decisions independently of any consideration of the cultural
traditions from which these works and thoughts stem. Evi-
dently, it was with this goal in mind that Bellow allegedly
made his offensive remark, and it is with this same goal in
mind that Taylor's reply condemns it.

My aim has not been to dispute the propriety of this goal
in education or of Taylor's remarks about the implications
that our newly developing recognition of non-Western, non-
European, nonwhite cultures has for our ideas about how to
attain it. Rather, it has been to point out that this is not, nor
has it ever been, the only legitimate goal of education. Learning to think rigorously and creatively, to look and listen sen-

sitively and with an open mind, have always been educational goals that are pursued through a variety of methods of which exposure to great works is but one. More to the point, learning to understand *ourselves, our* history, *our* environment, *our* language, *our* political system (and the history, culture, language, and politics of societies of particular interest or proximity to us), have always been goals whose justification and value are not disputed.

Until recently, perhaps, whites descended from Europe have not felt the need to sort out what reasons they (or we) had for wanting to study and to teach their literature and their history. The politics of recognition has increased their sensitivity to the fact that *their* literature might not be coextensive with great literature. Recognizing this gives us occasion to wonder what does explain and justify their interest in and commitment to studying Shakespeare, for example— is it his sheer objective, transcultural greatness or his importance in defining and shaping our literary and dramatic traditions? In the case of Shakespeare, I should think, there is no need to choose. Both are perfectly good reasons for studying Shakespeare, for including Shakespeare in the curriculum. More generally, both *types* of reason that these singular reasons exemplify have their place in educational decision-making. Both forms of justification are affected by a conscientious recognition of cultural diversity.

Taylor, following Bellow's lead, is concerned with the first type of justification. He takes it for granted that one's reason for studying one culture rather than another must be that that culture is of particular objective importance, or that it has some especially valuable aesthetic or intellectual contribution to make. Taylor is right to note that the values reflected in this type of reason also give us reason to search the world over, with patience and with care, to find and learn to appreciate great human achievements, wherever they may be.

Taylor's reason for studying different cultures, then, is that over time these studies are very likely to "pay off" in terms of an enlarged understanding of the world and a heightened sensitivity to beauty. This is *a* reason for studying different cultures, to be sure, but it is not the only reason, nor, I think, is it the most pressing one.

My point in this essay is to acknowledge the legitimacy of the second type of justification, but to insist that in this context, at least as much as in the former one, there is a need for a conscientious recognition of cultural diversity. Indeed, in this context, we might even say that justice requires it.

There is nothing wrong with having a special interest in a culture because it is one's own, or because it is the culture of one's friend or one's spouse. Indeed, having a special communal interest in one's own communal culture and one's own communal history is part of what keeps the communal culture alive, part of what creates, reforms, and sustains that culture. But the politics of recognition has consequences for what is justified on these grounds that are at least as important as its consequences for what can be justified impartially. The politics of recognition urges us not just to make efforts to recognize the other more actively and accurately—to recognize those people and those cultures that occupy the world in addition to ourselves—it urges us also to take a closer, less selective look at who is sharing the cities, the libraries, the schools we call our own. There is nothing wrong with allotting a special place in the curriculum for the study of our history, our literature, our culture. But if we are to study our culture, we had better recognize who we, as a community, are.

Comment

STEVEN C. ROCKEFELLER

THE LIBERAL DEMOCRATIC tradition has been formed by an ideal of universal freedom, equality, and fulfillment, which even in the best situations has been only partially realized and which may not yet be fully imagined. The spiritual meaning of American history and the history of other democratic nations is chiefly the story of the quest for this ideal. The heart of the liberal tradition is a creative process, a social and individual method of transformation, designed to enable men and women to pursue the embodiment of this ideal. Charles Taylor has made clear the way multiculturalism and the politics of difference and equal recognition are currently influencing this process of transformation. He has explained in a most instructive fashion the historical origins in modern thought of ideas that are playing a central role in the current debate over these matters.

At a minimum, the politics and ethics of equal dignity need to be deepened and expanded so that respect for the individual is understood to involve not only respect for the universal human potential in every person but also respect for the intrinsic value of the different cultural forms in and through which individuals actualize their humanity and express their unique personalities. The following reflections endeavor to put this idea in perspective by considering the politics of equal recognition in relation to the values of liberal democracy, the environmental movement, and the religious dimension of experience. These perspectives can help us to

87

appreciate the positive contributions of the politics of recognition and to clarify the dangers in the extreme forms of it that threaten to subvert the ideals of universal freedom and inclusive community.

I

First of all, it is important to clarify a basic issue when discussing recognition of diversity in a democratic social and political context. From the democratic point of view, a person's ethnic identity is not his or her primary identity, and important as respect for diversity is in multicultural democratic societies, ethnic identity is not the foundation of recognition of equal value and the related idea of equal rights. All human beings as the bearers of a universal human nature— as persons—are of equal value from the democratic perspective, and all people as persons deserve equal respect and equal opportunity for self-realization. In other words, from the liberal democratic point of view a person has a right to claim equal recognition first and foremost on the basis of his or her universal human identity and potential, not primarily on the basis of an ethnic identity. Our universal identity as human beings is our primary identity and is more fundamental than any particular identity, whether it be a matter of citizenship, gender, race, or ethnic origin.

It may be that in some situations the rights of individuals can best be defended by addressing the rights of an entire group defined, for example, by gender or race, but this does not alter the situation regarding a person's primary identity. To elevate ethnic identity, which is secondary, to a position equal in significance to, or above, a person's universal identity is to weaken the foundations of liberalism and to open the door to intolerance.

What is universally shared in human nature expresses itself in a great diversity of cultural forms. From the democratic perspective, particular cultures are critically evaluated in the light of the way they give distinct concrete expression to universal capacities and values. The objective of a liberal democratic culture is to respect—not to repress—ethnic identities and to encourage different cultural traditions to develop fully their potential for expression of the democratic ideals of freedom and equality, leading in most cases to major cultural transformations. How diverse cultures accomplish this task will vary, giving a rich variety worldwide to the forms of democratic life. Cultures can undergo significant intellectual, social, moral, and religious changes while maintaining continuity with their past.

These reflections raise some questions about Taylor's endorsement of a model of liberalism that allows the goals of a particular cultural group, such as the French Canadians in Quebec, to be actively supported by government in the name of cultural survival. It is one thing to support on the basis of the right to self-determination the political autonomy of a historically distinct and autonomous group such as a Stone Age tribal people in New Guinea or Tibetan Buddhist culture in China. The situation gets more complicated when one is considering creation of an autonomous state within a democratic nation as in the case of the Quebeckers or establishment of a separate public school system with its own curriculum for a particular group in the United States. Regarding Taylor's Quebec brand of liberalism, I am uneasy about the danger of an erosion over time of fundamental human rights growing out of a separatist mentality that elevates ethnic identity over universal human identity. American democracy has developed as an endeavor to transcend the separatism and ethnic rivalries that have had such a destructive effect on life in the "old world," the Yugoslavian civil war being only the most recent example.

II

Clarification of the nature and meaning of liberal democracy provides a way to explore further the moral and political issues raised by the politics of recognition. Some contemporary liberals have argued for a view of the liberal state as neutral between conceptions of the good life. Procedural liberalism in this view involves a moral commitment to processes that ensure the fair and equal treatment of all but not a moral commitment to specific ends of life, that is, an idea of the good life. For example, procedural liberalism respects the separation of church and state. It is also argued that procedural liberalism creates a kind of universal culture in which all groups can flourish and live together. However, many multiculturalists today challenge the idea that liberalism can be neutral with regard to conceptions of the good life, arguing that it reflects a regional Anglo-American culture and has a homogenizing effect. They reject the view that liberalism is or can be a universal culture.

There is some truth in both of these interpretations of liberalism. A liberal political culture is neutral in the sense that it promotes tolerance and protects freedom of conscience, religion, speech, and assembly in a way that no other culture does. Liberalism at its best also represents a universal human aspiration for individual freedom and self-expression as no other culture does. However, this is only part of the story. As Taylor recognizes, liberalism is "a fighting creed" and "can't and shouldn't claim complete cultural neutrality." What is this "fighting creed"? What is the meaning of liberal democracy? Taylor has not articulated it as fully as John Dewey.

A variety of Americans, for different reasons, endorse the idea of a purely procedural form of political liberalism in the belief that it is morally neutral regarding conceptions of the good life. However, they miss the full moral meaning of liberal democracy, which contains within it a substantive idea of the good life. Liberalism, as Dewey argued, is the expression of a distinct moral faith and way of life.[1]

For liberals like Dewey, the good life is a process, a way of living, of interacting with the world, and of solving problems, that leads to ongoing individual growth and social transformation. One realizes the end of life, the good life, each and every day by living with a liberal spirit, showing equal respect to all citizens, preserving an open mind, practicing tolerance, cultivating a sympathetic interest in the needs and struggles of others, imagining new possibilities, protecting basic human rights and freedoms, solving problems with the method of intelligence in a nonviolent atmosphere pervaded by a spirit of cooperation. These are primary among the liberal democratic virtues.

Liberal democracy, from this Deweyan viewpoint, is not first and foremost a political mechanism; it is a way of individual life. Liberal democratic politics are strong and healthy only when a whole society is pervaded by the spirit of democracy—in the family, in the school, in business and industry, and in religious institutions as well as in political institutions. The moral meaning of democracy is found in reconstructing all institutions so that they become instruments of human growth and liberation. This is why issues of child abuse and sexual harassment, as well as discrimination on the basis of gender, race, or sexual orientation, are liberal democratic issues.

Liberal democracy is a social strategy for enabling individuals to live the good life. It is unalterably opposed to ignorance. It trusts that knowledge and understanding have the power to set people free. Its lifeblood is free communication building on freedom of inquiry, speech, and assembly. The

---

[1] See, for example, John Dewey, "Creative Democracy—The Task Before Us," in *Later Works of John Dewey, 1925–1935*, ed. Jo Ann Boydston (Carbondale: Southern Illinois University Press, 1988), 14:224–30.

liberating power of democracy is also closely tied to what one might call the democratic method of truth, which relies on experience and experimental intelligence. The idea of moral absolutes and a fixed hierarchy of values is rejected. No idea of the good is above criticism, but this does not lead to a directionless relativism. Through experience with the aid of experimental intelligence, one can find ample grounds for making objective value judgments in any particular situation.

When a liberal society faces the question of granting special privileges, immunities, and political autonomy to one cultural group such as the French Canadians in Quebec, it cannot compromise on fundamental human rights, as Professor Taylor acknowledges. Furthermore, those who understand liberal democracy as itself a way of life grounded in a distinct moral faith cannot in good conscience agree to allow schools or the government to suppress the democratic way of growth and transformation. The democratic way conflicts with any rigid idea of, or absolute right to, cultural survival. The democratic way means respect for and openness to all cultures, but it also challenges all cultures to abandon those intellectual and moral values that are inconsistent with the ideals of freedom, equality, and the ongoing cooperative experimental search for truth and well-being. It is a creative method of transformation. This is its deeper spiritual and revolutionary significance.

Taylor indicates appreciation of this significance when he describes the value of a cross-cultural dialogue that transforms human understanding, leading to a "fusion of horizons." However, it is unlikely that a society will be open to such a transformation if it is preoccupied with the protection of one particular culture to the extent of allowing the government to maintain that culture at the expense of individual freedom. There is an uneasy tension here between Taylor's defense of the political principle of cultural survival and his espousal of open-minded cross-cultural exchange. As liberal democracies wrestle today with the problems identified by the politics of difference and make adjustments in response to powerful separatist and nationalistic forces, it is essential that they not lose sight of this issue.

III

Taylor considers at some length the question of how and on what basis different cultural groups are to be recognized and respected. In this regard, it is instructive to note the emergence of a politics of recognition with the environmental movement as well as with the politics of difference and multiculturalism. The environmentalists demand a respect for animals, trees, rivers, and ecosystems. They, like the multiculturalists, are concerned with a new appreciation of diversity and with the moral and legal standing of the rights of oppressed groups. Furthermore, just as multiculturalists might criticize the positing of the achievements of one group, such as white European and American males, as the norm of fully developed humanity, so some environmentalists criticize an anthropocentric outlook that posits human beings as the final end of the creation process and as inherently superior to all other beings. In both cases there is an attack on hierarchical modes of thought that tend to diminish or deny the value of other beings.

In an attempt to address this issue, many environmentalists abandon an anthropocentric orientation that views nonhuman life forms as possessing instrumental value only and as existing solely as a means to human ends. They embrace a biocentric perspective that affirms the inherent value of all life forms. For example, the United Nations World Charter for Nature, which was approved by the General Assembly in 1982, includes the principle that "every form of life is unique, warranting respect regardless of its worth to man," and it goes on to assert that human beings have a moral obligation to respect all life forms.

This line of thinking can be applied to the question of the value of diverse human cultures. (In line with Taylor's definition, the concern here is with "cultures that have animated whole societies over some considerable stretch of time.") It may be argued that human cultures are themselves like life forms. They are the products of natural evolutionary processes of organic growth. Each, in its own distinct fashion, reveals the way the creative energy of the universe, working through human nature in interaction with a distinct environment, has come to a unique focus. Each has its own place in the larger scheme of things, and each possesses intrinsic value quite apart from whatever value its traditions may have for other cultures. This fact is not altered by the consideration that, like living beings, cultures may develop into disintegrated and diseased forms.

Just as some deep ecologists embrace a biocentric egalitarianism, so some multiculturalists demand that all cultures receive recognition of equal value. Drawing on the insights of modern social psychology, Taylor has presented a persuasive argument for a new moral attitude that involves approaching all cultures with at least a presumption of equal value. One is reminded of the ancient rabbinic saying that a "wise person learns from everyone." Taylor's proposal seems entirely consistent with the liberal democratic spirit. However, the idea of a presumption of equal value involves the view that upon close scrutiny some cultures may not be found to be of equal value. Taylor's resistance to an outright judgment of equal value reflects a critical perspective that is concerned with the progressive evolution of civilization and the need to make distinctions about the relative merits of various achievements of different cultures. However, the ecological standpoint offers another perspective in light of which all cultures possess intrinsic value and in this sense are of equal value. Both perspectives have their place and are not mutually exclusive.

Translated into programs of responsible action, a presumption, or recognition, of equal value means, for example, rewriting basic textbooks for our schools, as has been done in California and is being done in New York. However, I share the concerns expressed by Arthur Schlesinger, Jr., that such undertakings not create increased social fragmentation.[2] We need a new, deeper appreciation of the ethnic histories of the American people, not a reduction of American history to ethnic histories.

IV

Taylor states that there may be a religious ground for a presumption of the equal worth of different cultures, and it is illuminating to consider the question of recognition of equal value from a religious perspective. The arguments in defense of the idea of equal dignity in Western democracies continue to reflect the influence of the ancient biblical and classical Greek notions that there is something sacred about human personality. Likewise, in the defense of the idea of the intrinsic value of all life forms, which is put forth by environmentalists, one frequently encounters thinking that has roots in religious experience and beliefs. All life is sacred, is the claim. All of the various forms of life are ends in themselves, and none should be viewed as a means only. In the language of Martin Buber, all life forms should be respected as a "thou" and not just as an "it." As Albert Schweitzer put it, one should respect the life in all beings as sacred and practice reverence for all life. Some ecological thinkers like Aldo Leo-

[2] Arthur Schlesinger, Jr., "A Dissenting Opinion," *Report of the Social Studies Syllabus Review Committee*, State Education Department, State University of New York, Albany, N.Y., 13 June 1991, p. 89.

pold have tried to give the idea of the moral rights of nature a scientific and secular defense, but the idea of the sacred is usually implicit or not far in the background.

If, as has been suggested, all cultures as well as all life forms are of intrinsic value and also sacred, then from a religious perspective all are in this sense equal in value. The fourteenth-century Christian mystic Meister Eckhart asserted: "God loves all creatures equally and fills them with his being. And we should lovingly meet all creatures in the same way."[3] In the spirit of Johann Gottfried Herder's outlook, which is cited by Taylor, Aleksandr Solzhenitsyn writes: "Every people, even the very smallest, represents a unique facet of God's design." Solzhenitsyn goes on to cite Vladimir Solovyov's reconstruction of the second great commandment: " 'You must love all other people as you love your own.' "[4]

If one employs this kind of religious argument in defense of the idea of equal value, one should recognize its full implications. It is opposed to anthropocentrism as well as to all egoisms of class, race, or culture. It calls for an attitude of humility. It encourages a respect for, and pride in, one's own particular identity only insofar as such respect and pride grow out of a recognition of the value of the uniqueness in the identity of all other peoples and life forms. Furthermore, if what is sacred in humanity is life, which is not something exclusively human, then humanity's primary identity is not just with the human species but with the entire biosphere that envelops planet Earth. Questions concerning equal dignity, respect for ethnic diversity, and cultural survival should be explored, therefore, in a context that includes consideration of respect for nature.

[3] See Matthew Fox, *Breakthrough: Meister Eckhart's Creation Spirituality in New Translation* (Garden City, N.Y.: Doubleday, 1980), p. 92.

[4] Aleksandr Solzhenitsyn, *Rebuilding Russia: Reflections and Tentative Proposals*, trans. Alexis Klimoff (New York: Farrar, Straus & Giroux, 1991), p. 21.

Finally, we can gain further insight into the meaning of the demand for equal recognition by considering the psychological dimension of the issue. Some multiculturalists may demand recognition of equal value chiefly in order to gain leverage in pressing the political agenda of a particular minority group. However, there is more to multiculturalism than this. The call for recognition of the equal value of different cultures is the expression of a basic and profound universal human need for unconditional acceptance. A feeling of such acceptance, including affirmation of one's ethnic particularity as well as one's universally shared potential, is an essential part of a strong sense of identity. As Taylor points out, the formation of a person's identity is closely connected to positive social recognition—acceptance and respect—from parents, friends, loved ones, and also from the larger society. A highly developed sense of identity involves still more. Human beings need not only a sense of belonging in relation to human society. Especially when confronted with death, we also need an enduring sense of belonging to—of being a valued part of—the larger whole which is the universe. The politics of recognition may, therefore, also be an expression of a complex human need for acceptance and belonging, which on the deepest level is a religious need. To offer only a presumption of equal value does not fully address this deeper human need. Moreover, from a cosmic perspective, all peoples together with their diverse cultures may well possess inherent value and belong in some ultimate sense. This may be the element of truth in the idea of equal value from a religious perspective.

It is not possible for secular politics to address fully the religious needs of individuals or groups for a sense of unconditional acceptance. However, any liberal democratic politics committed to the ideals of freedom and equality cannot escape the demand that it create inclusive and sustaining social environments that respect all peoples in their cultural diversity, giving them a feeling of belonging to the larger community. Furthermore, insofar as a liberal democracy encourages people to identify not only with their ethnic group or nation but also with humanity and other life forms more generally, it also nurtures a spiritual orientation conducive to realization of a sense of harmony with the cosmos.

If an affirmation of equal value is made on ecological or religious grounds, this does not diminish the importance of in-depth critical appraisal of the achievements and practices of different cultures. Comparative study and critical analysis are essential to the development of cross-cultural understanding and progressive social reconstruction. In a liberal democracy such work can and should be carried on, however, within a framework of mutual respect founded on recognition of the intrinsic worth of all cultures.

❖

Comment

MICHAEL WALZER

Iﬀ the purpose of commentary is disagreement (that being one of the human values that we mean to defend), then I am bound to be a poor commentator. For I not only admire the historical and philosophical style of Charles Taylor's essay, I am entirely in agreement with the views that he presents. So I shall try simply to raise a question from within his own argument, standing as best I can where he is standing—in opposition to a certain sort of high-minded moral absolutism and also to a certain sort of low-minded (he calls it neo-Nietzschean) subjectivism.

My question is about the two kinds of liberalism that Taylor has described and that I shall redescribe, abbreviating his account. (1) The first kind of liberalism ("Liberalism 1") is committed in the strongest possible way to individual rights and, almost as a deduction from this, to a rigorously neutral state, that is, a state without cultural or religious projects or, indeed, any sort of collective goals beyond the personal freedom and the physical security, welfare, and safety of its citizens. (2) The second kind of liberalism ("Liberalism 2") allows for a state committed to the survival and flourishing of a particular nation, culture, or religion, or of a (limited) set of nations, cultures, and religions—so long as the basic rights of citizens who have different commitments or no such commitments at all are protected.

Taylor prefers the second of these liberalisms, though he does not defend this preference at length in his essay. It is important to notice that Liberalism 2 is permissive, not determinate: liberals of the second kind, Taylor writes, "are willing to weigh the importance of certain forms of uniform treatment [in accordance with a strong theory of rights] against the importance of cultural survival, and opt *sometimes* [my emphasis] in favor of the latter." This obviously means that liberals of the second kind will opt sometimes in favor of liberalism of the first kind. Liberalism 2 is optional, and one of the options is Liberalism 1.

This sounds right to me. We don't make singular or once-and-for-all choices here; we adapt our politics to fit our circumstances, even if we also want to modify or transform our circumstances. But—this is my question—when should we choose this way or that way, Liberalism 1 or Liberalism 2?

Taylor's Canadian example nicely poses and perhaps answers this question. He would, I gather, make the exception that the Quebeckers want, recognizing Quebec as a "distinct society" and allowing the provincial government to choose Liberalism 2 and then to act (within limits: it can require French signage; it cannot ban English newspapers) for the preservation of French culture. But this is precisely to *make an exception*; the federal government would not itself take on this Quebecan project or any other of a similar sort. Vis-à-vis all the ethnicities and religions of Canada, it remains neutral; it defends, that is, a liberalism of the first kind.

Most liberal nation-states (think of Norway, France, and the Netherlands as examples) are more like Quebec than Canada. Their governments take an interest in the cultural survival of the majority nation; they don't claim to be neutral with reference to the language, history, literature, calendar, or even the minor mores of the majority. To all these they accord public recognition and support, with no visible anxiety. At the same time, they vindicate their liberalism by tolerating and respecting ethnic and religious differences and allowing all minorities an equal freedom to organize their members, express their cultural values, and reproduce their way of life in civil society and in the family.

All nation-states act to reproduce men and women of a certain sort: Norwegian, French, Dutch, or whatever. I don't doubt that there is tension, sometimes open conflict, between these official efforts at social reproduction and the unofficial efforts of minorities to sustain themselves over time. Tension and conflict seem to be inherent in Liberalism 2, but that is not a reason to reject it—not in those places where it fits the needs of a long-established majority nation. Nor can the conflict be avoided by requiring the Norwegian state, say, to provide the same kind of support to minority groups as it provides for the majority. For it could hardly do that without segregating the various minorities and giving them control of their own public space, carving out a Quebec, as it were, or a number of Quebecs, on its own soil, where none exist. And what possible reason could it have for adopting any such policy? Liberalism 2 is entirely appropriate here, as it is appropriate in the actual Quebec. There doesn't seem to be any requirement of equal provision or equal protection for minority cultures, so long as basic rights are respected.

The first sort of liberalism, by contrast, is the official doctrine of immigrant societies like the United States (and federal Canada too), and it also seems entirely appropriate to its time and place. For the United States isn't, after all, a nation-state, but a nation of nationalities, as Horace Kallen wrote in the second decade of our century, or a social union of social unions, in John Rawls's more recent formulation. Here the singular union claims to distinguish itself from all the plural unions, refusing to endorse or support their ways of life or to take an active interest in their social reproduction or to allow any one of them to seize state power, even locally. Given the absence of strong territorially based minorities, the American union has never faced a "Quebecan" challenge. The plural unions are free to do the best they can on their own behalf. But they get no help from the state; they are all, equally, at risk. So far as Liberalism 1 is concerned, there is no privileged majority and there are no exceptional minorities.

This is the official doctrine. No doubt state neutrality is often hypocritical, always (for reasons Taylor makes clear) incomplete. Some nationalities or social unions or cultural communities are more at risk than others. The public culture of American life is more supportive, say, of this way of life than of that. For these people survival is more of a problem than for those. This is not only a matter of history and numbers but also of wealth and power. Hence the contemporary politics of "multiculturalism," which is in one of its forms a demand to defy wealth and power and equalize the risks. I am not sure how this can be done, but it is in principle at least compatible with Liberalism 1, that is to say, with a neutral state that takes no responsibility for anyone's (cultural) survival.

But multiculturalism is in another of its forms a demand to minimize the risks for all the nationalities, social unions, and cultural communities. Now the state is called upon to take responsibility for everyone's (cultural) survival. This is liberalism of the second kind, except that the "allowance" that Taylor suggests for official projects like that of the Quebeckers is here turned into a requirement. Once again, I do not know what state policies this would in fact require. What would the state have to do to guarantee or even to begin to guarantee the survival of all the minorities that make up American society? It would surely have to move beyond official recognition of the equal value of the different ways of life. The various minority groups would need control over public monies, segregated or partially segregated schools, employment quotas that encouraged people to register with this or that group, and so on.

Faced with such a prospect, my own inclination (and, I would guess, Taylor's too) would be to retreat to a liberalism of the first kind—for us, not for everyone: Liberalism 1 chosen from within Liberalism 2. *From within*: that means that the choice is not governed by an absolute commitment to state neutrality and individual rights—nor by the deep dislike of particularist identities (short of citizenship) that is common among liberals of the first sort. It is governed instead by the social condition and the actual life choices of *these* men and women.

Indeed, I would choose Liberalism 1 in part, at least, because I think that immigrants to societies like this one have already made the same choice. They intended (and still intend), were prepared (and still are prepared), to take cultural risks when they came here and to leave the certainties of their old way of life behind. No doubt, there are moments of sorrow and regret when they realize how much they have left behind. Nonetheless, the communities they have created here are different from those they knew before precisely in this sense, that they are adapted to, shaped significantly by, the liberal idea of individual rights. We would have to curtail these rights in crucial ways, far beyond anything required in Norway or even Quebec, if we were to treat our minorities as endangered species in need of official sponsorship and protection.

So, from inside Liberalism 2, weighing equal rights and cultural survival, as Taylor suggests we can and should do, I would opt for Liberalism 1—here, not everywhere. I see no reason why a liberalism of this kind could not support schools in which the study of otherness, especially of all the local othernesses, was pursued in the deeply serious way called for in Taylor's essay. Indeed, what other kind of liberalism, or antiliberalism, could possibly provide this support, encouraging people to study the culture of the other before the future of their own is guaranteed?

PART TWO

✤

‡

Struggles for Recognition in the
Democratic Constitutional State

JÜRGEN HABERMAS

Translated by Shierry Weber Nicholsen

M ODERN constitutions owe their existence to a conception found in modern natural law according to which citizens come together voluntarily to form a legal community of free and equal consociates. The constitution puts into effect precisely those rights that those individuals must grant one another if they want to order their life together legitimately by means of positive law. This conception presupposes the notion of individual [*subjektive*] rights and individual legal persons as the bearers of rights. While modern law establishes a basis for state-sanctioned relations of intersubjective recognition, the rights derived from them protect the vulnerable integrity of legal subjects who are in every case individuals. In the final analysis it is a question of protecting these individual legal persons, even if the integrity of the individual—in law no less than in morality—depends on relations of mutual recognition remaining intact. Can a theory of rights that is so individualistically constructed deal adequately with struggles for recognition in which it is the articulation and assertion of collective identities that seems to be at stake?

A constitution can be thought of as an historical project that each generation of citizens continues to pursue. In the democratic constitutional state the exercise of political power is coded in a dual manner: the institutionalized handling of problems and the procedurally regulated mediation of interests must simultaneously be understandable as actualizing a system of rights.[1] But in the political arena those who encounter one another are collective actors contending about collective goals and the distribution of collective goods. Only in the courtroom and in legal discourse are rights asserted and defended as actionable individual rights that can be sued for. Existing law also has to be interpreted in new ways in different contexts in view of new needs and new interests. This struggle over the interpretation and satisfaction of historically unredeemed claims is a struggle for legitimate rights in which collective actors are once again involved, combatting a lack of respect for their dignity. In this "struggle for recognition" collective experiences of violated integrity are articulated, as Axel Honneth has shown.[2] Can these phenomena be reconciled with a theory of rights that is individualistically designed?

The political achievements of liberalism and social democracy that are the product of the bourgeois emancipation movements and the European labor movement suggest an affirmative answer to this question. To be sure, both attempted to overcome the disenfranchisement of underprivileged groups and with it the division of society into social classes; but where liberal social reform came into play, the struggle against the oppression of collectivities deprived of equal social opportunities took the form of a struggle for the social-welfarist universalization of civil rights. Since the bankruptcy of state socialism, this perspective has indeed been the only one remaining: the status of a dependent wage earner is to be supplemented with rights to social and political participation, and the mass of the population is thereby to be given the opportunity to live in realistic expectation of security, social justice, and affluence. A more equitable dis-

---

[1] Jürgen Habermas, *Faktizität und Geltung* (Frankfurt am Main: Suhrkamp, 1992), chap. 3; English translation by William Rehq forthcoming (Cambridge, Mass.: MIT Press, 1994).

[2] Axel Honneth, *Kampf um Anerkennung* (Frankfurt am Main: Suhrkamp, 1992); English translation by Joel Andersen forthcoming (New York: Polity Press, 1994).

tribution of collective goods is to compensate for the unequal conditions of life in capitalist societies. This aim is thoroughly compatible with the theory of rights, because the primary goods (in Rawls's sense) are either distributed among individuals (like money, free time, and services) or used by individuals (like the infrastructures of transportation, health care, and education), and can thus take the form of individual claims to benefits.

At first glance, however, claims to the recognition of collective identities and to equal rights for cultural forms of life are a different matter. Feminists, minorities in multicultural societies, peoples struggling for national independence, and formerly colonized regions suing for the equality of their cultures on the international stage are all currently fighting for such claims. Does not the recognition of cultural forms of life and traditions that have been marginalized, whether in the context of a majority culture or in a Eurocentric global society, require guarantees of status and survival—in other words, some kind of collective rights that shatter the outmoded self-understanding of the democratic constitutional state, which is tailored to individual rights and in that sense is "liberal"?

In his contribution to this volume, Charles Taylor gives us a complex answer to this question, an answer that advances the discussion significantly.[3] As the commentaries on his essay published here indicate, his original ideas also inspire criticism. Taylor remains ambiguous on the decisive point. He distinguishes two readings of the democratic constitutional state, for which Michael Walzer provides the terms Liberalism 1 and Liberalism 2. These designations suggest that the second reading, which Taylor favors, merely corrects an inappropriate understanding of liberal principles. On closer examination, however, Taylor's reading attacks the principles themselves and calls into question the individualistic core of the modern conception of freedom.

[3] In this volume, pp. 25–73.

TAYLOR'S "POLITICS OF RECOGNITION"

Amy Gutmann makes the incontrovertible point that

> full public recognition as equal citizens may require two forms
> of respect: (1) respect for the unique identities of each individ-
> ual, regardless of gender, race, or ethnicity, and (2) respect
> for those activities, practices, and ways of viewing the world
> that are particularly valued by, or associated with, members
> of disadvantaged groups, including women, Asian-Ameri-
> cans, African-Americans, Native Americans, and a multitude
> of other groups in the United States.[4]

The same thing holds, of course, for *Gastarbeiter* [foreign
workers] and other foreigners in Germany, for Croats in Ser-
bia, Russians in the Ukraine, and Kurds in Turkey; for the
disabled, homosexuals, and so on. The demand for respect is
aimed not so much at equalizing living conditions as it is at
protecting the integrity of the traditions and forms of life in
which members of groups that have been discriminated
against can recognize themselves. Normally, of course, the
failure of cultural recognition is connected with gross social
discrimination, and the two reinforce each other. The question that concerns us here is whether the demand for the second kind of respect follows from the first, that is, from the
principle of equal respect for each individual, or whether, at
least in some cases, these two demands will necessarily
come into conflict with one another.

Taylor proceeds on the assumption that the protection of
collective identities comes into competition with the right to
equal individual [*subjektive*] liberties—Kant's one original
human right—so that in the case of conflict a decision must
be made about which takes precedence over the other. The
argument runs as follows: Because the second claim requires
consideration of precisely those particularities from which

---

[4] In this volume, p. 8.

the first claim seems to abstract, the principle of equal rights has to be put into effect in two kinds of politics that run counter to one another—a politics of consideration of cultural differences on the one hand and a politics of universalization of individual rights on the other. The one is supposed to compensate for the price the other exacts with its equalizing universalism. Taylor spells out this opposition—an opposition that is falsely construed, as I will try to show—using the concepts of the good and the just, drawn from moral theory. Liberals like Rawls and Dworkin call for an ethically neutral legal order that is supposed to assure everyone equal opportunity to pursue his or her own conception of the good. In contrast, communitarians like Taylor and Walzer dispute the ethical neutrality of the law and thus can expect the constitutional state, if need be, actively to advance specific conceptions of the good life.

Taylor gives the example of the French-speaking minority that forms the majority in the Canadian province of Quebec. The francophone group claims the right for Quebec to form a "distinct society" within the nation as a whole. It wants to safeguard the integrity of its form of life against the Anglo-Saxon majority culture by means, among other things, of regulations that forbid immigrants and the French-speaking population to send their children to English-language schools, that establish French as the language in which firms with more than fifty employees will operate, and that in general prescribe French as the language of business. According to Taylor, a theory of rights of the first type would necessarily be closed to collective goals of this kind:

> A society with collective goals like Quebec's violates this model.... On this model, there is a dangerous overlooking of an essential boundary in speaking of fundamental rights to things like commercial signage in the language of one's choice. One has to distinguish the fundamental liberties, those that should never be infringed and therefore ought to be unassailably entrenched, on one hand, from privileges and

111

immunities that are important, but that can be revoked or restricted for reasons of public policy—although one would need a strong reason to do this—on the other.[5]

Taylor proposes an alternative model that under certain conditions would permit basic rights to be restricted by guarantees of status aimed at promoting the survival of endangered cultural forms of life, and thus would permit policies that "actively seek to *create* members of the community, for instance, in their assuring that future generations continue to identify as French-speakers. There is no way that these policies could be seen as just providing a facility to already existing people."[6]

Taylor makes the case for his thesis of incompatibility by presenting the theory of rights in the selective reading of Liberalism 1. He does not clearly define either the Canadian example or the legal reference of his problematic. Before I take up these two problems, I would like to show that when properly understood the theory of rights is by no means blind to cultural differences.

Taylor understands Liberalism 1 as a theory according to which all legal consociates are guaranteed equal individual freedoms of choice and action in the form of basic rights. In cases of conflict the courts decide who has which rights; thus the principle of equal respect for each person holds only in the form of a legally protected autonomy that every person can use to realize his or her personal life project. This interpretation of the system of rights is paternalistic in that it ignores half of the concept of autonomy. It does not take into consideration that those to whom the law is addressed can acquire autonomy (in the Kantian sense) only to the extent that they can understand themselves to be the authors of the laws to which they are subject as private legal persons. Liberalism 1 fails to recognize that private and public autonomy

[5] Cf. Taylor, in this volume, pp. 58–59.
[6] In this volume, pp. 58–59.

are equiprimordial. It is not a matter of public autonomy supplementing and remaining external to private autonomy, but rather of an internal, that is, conceptually necessary connection between them. For in the final analysis, private legal persons cannot even attain the enjoyment of equal individual liberties unless they themselves, by jointly exercising their autonomy as citizens, arrive at a clear understanding about what interests and criteria are justified and in what respects equal things will be treated equally and unequal things unequally in any particular case.

Once we take this internal connection between democracy and the constitutional state seriously, it becomes clear that the system of rights is blind neither to unequal social conditions nor to cultural differences. The color-blindness of the selective reading vanishes once we assume that we ascribe to the bearers of individual rights an identity that is conceived intersubjectively. Persons, and legal persons as well, become individualized only through a process of socialization.[7] A correctly understood theory of rights requires a politics of recognition that protects the integrity of the individual in the life contexts in which his or her identity is formed. This does not require an alternative model that would correct the individualistic design of the system of rights through other normative perspectives. All that is required is the consistent actualization of the system of rights. There would be little likelihood of this, of course, without social movements and political struggles. We see this in the history of feminism, which has had to make repeated attempts to realize its legal and political goals in the face of strong resistance.

Like the development of law in Western societies in general, the feminist politics of equality during the past hundred years follows a pattern that can be described as a dialectic of

---

[7] Jürgen Habermas, "Individuation through Socialization," in Habermas, *Postmetaphysical Thinking*, translated by William Mark Hohengarten (Cambridge, Mass.: MIT Press, 1992), pp. 149–204.

de jure and *de facto* equality. Equality under the law grants freedoms of choice and action that can be used differently and thus do not promote actual equality in life circumstances or positions of power. Now, on the one hand, if the factual prerequisites for the equal opportunity to make use of equally distributed legal competence are not fulfilled, the normative meaning of legal equality will turn into its opposite. On the other hand, the intended equalization of actual life circumstances and positions of power should not lead to "normalizing" interventions that perceptibly restrict the capacities of the presumed beneficiaries to shape their lives autonomously. As long as policies are focused on safeguarding private autonomy, while the internal connection between the individual rights of private persons and the public autonomy of the citizens who participate in making the laws is obscured from view, the politics of rights will oscillate helplessly between the poles of a liberal paradigm in the Lockean sense and an equally shortsighted social-welfare paradigm. This is true of equal treatment for men and women as well.[8]

Initially, the goal of the liberal policies was to detach the acquisition of status from gender and to guarantee women equal opportunity to compete for jobs, social standing, education, political power, and so on, regardless of the outcomes. But the formal equality that was partially achieved thereby only made the *de facto* unequal treatment of women all the more obvious. Social-welfare policies, especially in the areas of social, labor, and family law, responded to this with special regulations regarding pregnancy, motherhood, and the social burdens of divorce. Since then, of course, not only unfulfilled liberal demands but also the ambivalent consequences of successfully implemented social-welfare programs have become the object of feminist criticism—for ex-

[8] Deborah L. Rhode, *Justice and Gender* (Cambridge, Mass.: Harvard University Press, 1989), Part 1.

ample, the increased employment risks that women suffer as a result of these compensations, the overrepresentation of women in the lower wage brackets, the problematic notion of "child welfare," the increasing "feminization" of poverty in general, and so on. From the legal point of view there is a structural basis for this reflexively produced discrimination, namely, the overgeneralized classifications of disadvantageous situations and disadvantaged groups. These "false" classifications lead to "normalizing" interventions into the way people lead their lives, with the result that the intended compensations turn into new forms of discrimination and instead of liberties being guaranteed people are deprived of freedom. In the domains of law that feminism is particularly concerned with, social-welfare paternalism is precisely that, because legislation and adjudication are oriented to traditional patterns of interpretation and thus serve only to strengthen existing gender stereotypes.

The classification of sex roles and gender-dependent differences touches fundamental levels of a society's cultural self-understanding. Radical feminism is only now making us aware of the fallible nature of this self-understanding, which is fundamentally debatable and in need of revision. Radical feminism rightly insists that the relevance of differences in experiences and life circumstances in (specific groups of) men and women with respect to equal opportunity to exercise individual liberties must be discussed in the political public sphere, in public debates about the appropriate interpretation of needs.[9] Hence this struggle for equality for women is a particularly good illustration of the need for a change in the paradigmatic understanding of rights. The debate about whether the autonomy of legal persons is better ensured through the individual freedom of private persons to compete or through objectively guaranteed claims to bene-

[9] Nancy Fraser, "Struggle over Needs," in Fraser, *Unruly Practices* (Minneapolis: University of Minnesota Press, 1989), pp. 144–60.

fits for clients of welfare-state bureaucracies is being replaced by a proceduralist conception of rights according to which the democratic process has to safeguard both private and public autonomy at the same time. The individual rights that are supposed to guarantee women the autonomy to shape their private lives cannot even be appropriately formulated unless those affected articulate and justify in public discussion what is relevant to equal or unequal treatment in typical cases. Safeguarding the private autonomy of citizens with equal rights must go hand in hand with activating their autonomy as citizens of the nation.

A "liberal" version of the system of rights that fails to take this connection into account will necessarily misunderstand the universalism of basic rights as an abstract levelling of distinctions, a levelling of both cultural and social differences. To the contrary, these differences must be seen in increasingly context-sensitive ways if the system of rights is to be actualized democratically. The process of universalizing civil rights continues to fuel the differentiation of the legal system, which cannot ensure the integrity of legal subjects without strict equal treatment, directed by the citizens themselves, of the life contexts that safeguard their identities. If the selective reading of the theory of rights is corrected to include a democratic understanding of the actualization of basic rights, there is no need to contrast a truncated Liberalism 1 with a model that introduces a notion of collective rights that is alien to the system.

STRUGGLES FOR RECOGNITION: THE PHENOMENA AND THE LEVELS OF THEIR ANALYSIS

Feminism, multiculturalism, nationalism, and the struggle against the Eurocentric heritage of colonialism are related phenomena that should not be confused with one another. They are related in that women, ethnic and cultural minori-

ties, and nations and cultures defend themselves against oppression, marginalization, and disrespect and thereby struggle for the recognition of collective identities, whether in the
context of a majority culture or within the community of peoples. We are concerned here with liberation movements
whose collective political goals are defined primarily in cultural terms, even though social and economic inequalities as
well as political dependencies are also always involved.

(a) *Feminism* is of course not a minority cause, but it is directed against a dominant culture that interprets the relationship of the sexes in an asymmetrical manner that excludes
equal rights. Gender-specific differences in life circumstances and experiences do not receive adequate consideration, either legally or informally. Women's cultural self-
understanding is not given due recognition, any more than
their contribution to the common culture; given the prevail-
ing definitions, women's needs cannot even be adequately
articulated. Thus the political struggle for recognition begins
as a struggle about the interpretation of gender-specific
achievements and interests. Insofar as it is successful, it
changes the relationship between the sexes along with the
collective identity of women, thereby directly affecting
men's self-understanding as well. The scale of values of the
society as a whole is up for discussion; the consequences of
this problematization extend into core private areas and af-
fect the established boundaries between the private and public spheres as well.[10]

(b) The struggle of *oppressed ethnic and cultural minorities* for
the recognition of their collective identities is a different matter. Since these liberation movements also aim at overcoming an illegitimate division of society, the majority culture's
self-understanding cannot remain untouched by them. But
from the point of view of members of the majority culture,
the revised interpretation of the achievements and interests

---

[10] Seyla Benhabib, *Situating the Self* (New York: Routledge, 1992), Part 2.

of others does not necessarily alter their own role in the same
way that the reinterpretation of the relations between the
sexes alters the role of men.

Liberation movements in multicultural societies are not a
uniform phenomenon. They present different challenges depending on whether it is a question of endogenous minorities becoming aware of their identity or new minorities arising through immigration, and depending on whether the
nations faced with the challenge have always understood
themselves to be countries open to immigration on the basis
of their history and political culture or whether the national
self-understanding needs first to be adjusted to accommodate the integration of alien cultures. The challenge becomes
all the greater, the more profound are the religious, racial, or
ethnic differences or the historical-cultural disjunctions to be
bridged. The challenge becomes all the more painful, the
more the tendencies to self-assertion take on a fundamentalist and separatist character, whether because experiences of
impotence lead the minority struggling for recognition to
take a regressive position or because the minority in question
has to use mass mobilization to awaken consciousness in
order to articulate a newly constructed identity.

(c) This differs from the *nationalism of peoples* who see
themselves as ethnically and linguistically homogeneous
groups against the background of a common historical fate
and who want to protect their identity not only as an ethnic
community but as a people forming a nation with the capacity for political action. Nationalist movements have almost
always modeled themselves on the republican nation-state
that emerged from the French Revolution. Compared with
the first generation of nation-states, Italy and Germany were
"belated nations." The period of decolonialization after the
Second World War represents yet another context. And the
constellations at the collapse of empires like the Ottoman
Empire, the Austro-Hungarian Empire, or the Soviet Union
were different still. The situation of national minorities like

the Basques, the Kurds, or the Northern Irish, which emerged in the course of the formation of nation-states, is again different. And the founding of the state of Israel is a special case, emerging from a national-religious movement and the horrors of Auschwitz, in the British Mandate of Palestine, which is claimed by Arabs.

(d) *Eurocentrism and the hegemony of Western culture* are in the last analysis catchwords for a struggle for recognition on the international level. The Gulf War made us aware of this. Under the shadow of a colonial history that is still vivid in people's minds, the allied intervention was regarded by religiously motivated masses and secularized intellectuals alike as a failure to respect the identity and autonomy of the Arabic-Islamic world. The historical relationship between the Occident and the Orient, and especially the relationship of the First to the former Third World, continues to bear the marks of a denial of recognition.

Even this cursory classification of the phenomena allows us to place the constitutional struggle between the Canadian government and Quebec on the borderline between (b) and (c). Below the threshold of a separatist move to found their own state, it is obvious that the French-speaking minority is struggling for rights that would be accorded them as a matter of course if they declared themselves to be an independent nation—as Croatia, Slovenia and Slovakia, the Baltic States, and Georgia have recently done. But they are aspiring to become a "state within a state," something for which a broad spectrum of federalist constructions is available, ranging from a federal state to a loose confederation. In Canada the decentralization of sovereign state powers is bound up with the question of cultural autonomy for a minority that would like to become the majority within its own house. New minorities would arise in turn, of course, with a change in the complexion of the majority culture.

In addition to distinguishing the phenomena categorized above, we need to distinguish different levels of their analysis. Taylor's remarks touch on at least three discourses to which these phenomena have given rise.

(e) In the debate about *political correctness* these phenomena served as an occasion for American intellectuals to engage in a process of self-reflection about the status of modernity.[11] Neither of the two parties to the debate wants to pursue the project of modernity on its own terms, as a project that should not be abandoned.[12] What the "radicals" see as an encouraging step into postmodernity and toward overcoming totalizing figures of thought is for the "traditionalists" the sign of a crisis that can be dealt with only through a return to the classical traditions of the West. We can leave this debate aside, since it contributes little to an analysis of struggles for recognition in the democratic constitutional state and virtually nothing to their political resolution.[13]

(f) The more strictly *philosophical discourses* that take these phenomena as a point of departure for describing general problems are on a different level. The phenomena are well suited to illustrate the difficulties of intercultural understanding. They illuminate the relationship of morality to ethical life [*Sittlichkeit*] or the internal connection between meaning and validity, and they provide new fuel for the old

[11] Paul Berman, ed., *Debating P.C.* (New York: Dell, 1992); see also J. Searle, "Storm over the University," in the same volume, pp. 85–123.

[12] Jürgen Habermas, *The Philosophical Discourse of Modernity*, translated by Frederick Lawrence (Cambridge, Mass.: MIT Press, 1987).

[13] As Amy Gutmann remarks of the deconstructionist method: "This reductionist argument about intellectual standards is often made on behalf of groups that are underrepresented in the university and disadvantaged in society, but it is hard to see how it can come to the aid of anyone. The argument is self-undermining, both logically and practically. By its internal logic, deconstructionism has nothing more to say for the view that intellectual standards are masks for the will to political power than that it too reflects the will to power of deconstructionists. But why then bother with intellectual life at all, which is not the fastest, surest, or even most satisfying path to political power, if it is political power that one is really after?" (this volume, pp. 18–19).

question of whether it is even possible to transcend the context of our own language and culture or whether all standards of rationality remain bound up with specific worldviews and traditions. The overwhelming evidence of the fragmentation of multicultural societies and the Babylonian confusion of tongues in an overly complex global society seems to impel us toward holistic conceptions of language and contextualist conceptions of worldviews that make us skeptical about universalist claims, whether cognitive or normative. The complex and still unsettled debate about rationality also has implications, of course, for the concepts of the good and the just with which we operate when we examine the conditions of a "politics of recognition." But Taylor's proposal itself has a different reference, which lies at the level of law and politics.

(g) The question of the *rights* of offended and disrespected minorities takes on a legal sense when it is posed in these terms. Political decisions must make use of the regulatory form of positive law to be at all effective in complex societies. In the medium of law, however, we are dealing with an artificial structure with certain normative presuppositions. Modern law is *formal*, because it rests on the premise that anything that is not explicitly forbidden is permitted. It is *individualistic*, because it makes the individual person the bearer of rights. It is *coercive*, because it is sanctioned by the state and applies only to legal or rule-conforming behavior— it permits the practice of religion but it cannot prescribe religious views. It is *positive* law, because it derives from the (modifiable) decisions of a political legislature; and finally, it is *procedurally enacted* law, because it is legitimated by a democratic process. Positive law requires purely legal behavior, but it must be legitimate; although it does not prescribe the motives for obeying the law, it must be such that its addressees can always obey it out of respect for the law. A legal order is legitimate when it safeguards the autonomy of all citizens to an equal degree. The citizens are autonomous only if the addressees of the law can also see themselves as its authors. And its authors are free only as participants in legislative processes that are regulated in such a way and take place in forms of communication such that everyone can presume that the regulations enacted in that way deserve general and rationally motivated assent. In normative terms, there is no such thing as a constitutional state without democracy. Since, on the other hand, the democratic process itself has to be legally institutionalized, the principle of popular sovereignty requires the fundamental rights without which there can be no legitimate law at all; first and foremost, the right to equal individual freedom of choice and action, which in turn presupposes comprehensive legal protection of individuals.

As soon as we treat a problem as a legal problem, we bring into play a conception of modern law that forces us—on conceptual grounds alone—to operate with the architectonics of the constitutional state and its wealth of presuppositions. This has implications for the way we deal with the problem of securing equal legal rights and equal recognition for groups that are culturally defined, that is, collectivities that are distinguished from other collectivities on the basis of tradition, forms of life, ethnic origins, and so on—and whose members want to be distinguished from all other collectivities in order to maintain and develop their identity.

The Permeation of the Constitutional State by Ethics

From the point of view of legal theory, the primary question that multiculturalism raises is the question of the ethical neutrality of law and politics. By "ethical" I mean all questions that relate to conceptions of the good life, or a life that is not misspent. Ethical questions cannot be evaluated from the "moral point of view" of whether something is "equally good for everyone"; rather, impartial judgment of such questions is based on strong evaluations and determined by the self-understanding and perspectival life-projects of particular groups, that is, by what is from their point of view "good for us," all things considered. The first-person reference, and hence the relationship to the identity of a group (or an individual) is grammatically inscribed in ethical questions. I will use the example of the Canadian constitutional debate to look at the liberal demand for ethical neutrality of the law in relation to the ethical-political self-understanding of a nation of citizens.

The neutrality of the law—and of the democratic process of enacting laws—is sometimes understood to mean that political questions of an ethical nature must be kept off the agenda and out of the discussion by "gag rules" because they are not susceptible of impartial legal regulation. On this view, in the sense of Liberalism 1, the state is not to be permitted to pursue any collective goals beyond guaranteeing the personal freedom and the welfare and security of its citizens. The alternative model (in the sense of Liberalism 2), in contrast, expects the state to guarantee these fundamental rights in general but beyond that also to intervene on behalf of the survival and advancement of a "particular nation, culture, religion, or of a (limited) set of nations, cultures and religions," in Michael Walzer's formulation. Walzer regards this model too as fundamental; it leaves room, however, for citizens to choose to give priority to individual rights under certain circumstances. Walzer shares Taylor's premise that conflicts between these two fundamental normative orientations are quite possible and that in such cases only Liberalism 2 permits collective goals and identities to be given precedence. Now, the theory of rights does in fact assert the absolute precedence of rights over collective goods, so that arguments about goals, as Dworkin shows, can only "trump" claims based on individual rights if these goals can in turn be justified in the light of other rights that take precedence.[14] But that alone is not sufficient to support the communitarian view, which Taylor and Walzer share, that the system of rights is blind to claims to the protection of cultural forms of life and collective identities and is thus "levelling" and in need of revision.

Earlier I used the example of the feminist politics of equality to make a general point, namely, that the democratic elaboration of a system of rights has to incorporate not only general political goals but also the collective goals that are articulated in struggles for recognition. For in distinction to the moral norms that regulate possible interactions between speaking and acting subjects in general, legal norms refer to the network of interactions in a specific society. Legal norms are derived from the decisions of a local lawmaking body and apply within a particular geographical area of the state to a socially delimited collectivity of members of that state. Within this well-defined sphere of validity, legal norms put the political decisions with which a society organized as a state acts upon itself into the form of collectively binding programs. To be sure, consideration of collective goals is not permitted to dissolve the structure of the law. It may not destroy the form of the law as such and thereby negate the difference between law and politics. But it is inherent in the concrete nature of the matters to be regulated that in the medium of law—as opposed to morality—the process of setting normative rules for modes of behavior is open to influence by the society's political goals. For this reason every legal system is also the expression of a particular form of life and not merely a reflection of the universal content of basic rights. Of course, legislative decisions must be understood as actualizing the system of rights, and policies must be understood as an elaboration of that system; but the more concrete the matter at hand, the more the self-understanding of

[14] Ronald Dworkin, *Taking Rights Seriously* (Cambridge, Mass.: Harvard University Press, 1977).

a collectivity and its form of life (as well as the balance between competing group interests and an informed choice between alternative ends and means) are expressed in the ac-
ceptability of the way the matter is legally regulated. We see
this in the broad spectrum of reasons that enter into the rational process by which the legislature's opinion and will are
formed: in addition to moral considerations, pragmatic considerations, and the results of fair negotiations, ethical reasons also enter into deliberations and justifications of legislative decisions.

To the extent to which the shaping of citizens' political
opinion and will is oriented to the idea of actualizing rights,
it cannot, as the communitarians suggest, be equated with a
process by which citizens reach agreement about their ethical-political self-understanding.[15] But the process of actualizing rights is indeed embedded in contexts that require such
discourses as an important component of politics—discussions about a shared conception of the good and a desired
form of life that is acknowledged to be authentic. In such discussions the participants clarify the way they want to understand themselves as citizens of a specific republic, as inhabitants of a specific region, as heirs to a specific culture, which
traditions they want to perpetuate and which they want to
discontinue, how they want to deal with their history, with
one another, with nature, and so on. And of course the
choice of an official language or a decision about the curriculum of public schools affects the nation's ethical self-
understanding. Because ethical-political decisions are an un-
avoidable part of politics, and because their legal regulation
expresses the collective identity of a nation of citizens, they
can spark cultural battles in which disrespected minorities
struggle against an insensitive majority culture. What sets
off the battles is not the ethical neutrality of the legal order

[15] Ronald Beiner, *Political Judgment* (Chicago: University of Chicago
Press, 1984), p. 138.

but rather the fact that every legal community and every democratic process for actualizing basic rights is inevitably permeated by ethics. We see evidence of this, for instance, in the institutional guarantees enjoyed by Christian churches in countries like Germany—despite freedom of religion—or in the recently challenged constitutional guarantee of status accorded the family in distinction to other marriage-like arrangements.

In this context it is interesting to note that both empirically and normatively such decisions depend on the composition of the citizenry of the nation-state, something that is contingent. The social make-up of the population of a state is the result of historical circumstances extrinsic to the system of rights and the principles of the constitutional state. It determines the totality of persons who live together in a territory and are bound by the constitution, that is, by the decision of the founding fathers to order their life together legitimately by means of positive law; their descendants have implicitly (and as naturalized citizens even explicitly) agreed to continue to pursue a preexisting constitutional project. Through their socialization processes, however, the persons of which a state is composed at any given time also embody the cultural forms of life in which they have developed their identity—even if they have become disengaged from the traditions of their origins. They form the nodal points, as it were, in an ascriptive network of cultures and traditions, of intersubjectively shared contexts of life and experience. And this network also forms the horizon within which the citizens of the nation, willingly or not, conduct the ethical-political discourses in which they attempt to reach agreement on their self-understanding. If the population of citizens as a whole shifts, this horizon will change as well; other discourses will be held about the same questions and other decisions will be reached. National minorities are at least intuitively aware of this, and it is an important motive for demanding their own state, or, as in the unsuccessful Meech Lake draft constitution, for demanding to be recognized as a "distinct society." If the francophone minority in Canada were to constitute itself as a legal community, it would form other majorities on important ethical-political questions through the same democratic processes and would arrive at regulatory decisions different from the ones Canadians as a whole have hitherto reached.[16]

As the history of the formation of nation-states shows, new national boundaries give rise to new national minorities. The problem does not disappear, except at the price of "ethnic cleansings"—a price that cannot be politically or morally justified. The double-edged nature of the "right" to national self-determination is clearly demonstrated in the case of the Kurds, who are spread across three different countries, or Bosnia-Herzegovina, where ethnic groups are battling one another mercilessly. On the one hand, a collectivity that thinks of itself as a community with its own identity attains a new level of recognition by taking the step of becoming a nation in its own right. It cannot reach this level as a pre-political linguistic and ethnic community, or even as an incorporated or a fragmented "cultural nation." The need to be recognized as a nation-state is intensified in times of crisis, when the populace clings to the ascriptive signs of a regressively revitalized collective identity, as for instance after the dissolution of the Soviet empire. This kind of support offers dubious compensation for well-founded fears about the future and lack of social stability. On the other hand, national independence is often to be had only at the price of civil wars, new kinds of repression, or ensuing problems that perpetuate the initial conflicts with the signs reversed.

The situation is different in Canada, where reasonable efforts are being made to find a federalist solution that will leave the nation as a whole intact but will try to safeguard

[16] Peter Alter, *Nationalism* (New York: Routledge, 1989).

the cultural autonomy of a part of it by decentralizing state powers. In this way the portion of the citizenry that participates in the democratic process in specific areas of policy will change, but the principles of that process will not. For the theory of rights in no way forbids the citizens of a democratic constitutional state to assert a conception of the good in their general legal order, a conception they either already share or have come to agree on through political discussion. It does, however, forbid them to privilege one form of life at the expense of others within the nation. In federal versions of the nation-state this is true at both the federal and the state levels. If I am not mistaken, in Canada the debate is not about this principle of equal rights but about the nature and extent of the state powers that are to be transferred to the Province of Quebec.

EQUAL RIGHTS TO COEXISTENCE VERSUS THE PRESERVATION OF SPECIES

Federalization is a possible solution only when members of different ethnic groups and cultural lifeworlds live in more or less separate geographical areas. In multicultural societies like the United States this is not the case. Nor will it be the case in countries like Germany, where the ethnic composition is changing under the pressure of global waves of migration. Even if Quebec became culturally autonomous, it would find itself in the same situation, having merely traded an English majority culture for a French one. If a well-functioning public sphere with open communication structures that permit and promote discussions oriented to self-understanding can develop in such multicultural societies against the background of a liberal culture and on the basis of voluntary associations, then the democratic process of actualizing equal individual rights will also extend to guaranteeing different ethnic groups and their cultural forms of life equal rights to coexistence. This does not require special justification or an alternative principle. For from a normative point of view, the integrity of the individual legal person cannot be guaranteed without protecting the intersubjectively shared experiences and life contexts in which the person has been socialized and has formed his or her identity. The identity of the individual is interwoven with collective identities and can be stabilized only in a cultural network that cannot be appropriated as private property any more than the mother tongue itself can be. Hence the individual remains the bearer of "rights to cultural membership," in Will Kymlicka's phrase.[17] But as the dialectic of legal and actual equality plays itself out, this gives rise to extensive guarantees of status, rights to self-administration, infrastructural benefits, subsidies, and so on. In arguing for their support, endangered indigenous cultures can advance special moral reasons arising from the history of a country that has been appropriated by the majority culture. Similar arguments in favor of "reverse discrimination" can be advanced for the long-suppressed and disavowed cultures of former slaves.[18]

These and similar obligations arise from legal claims and not from a general assessment of the value of the culture in question. Taylor's politics of recognition would not have much to stand on if it were dependent on the "presumption of equal value" of cultures and their contributions to world civilization. The right to equal respect, which everyone can demand in the life contexts in which his or her identity is formed as well as elsewhere, has nothing to do with the presumed excellence of his or her culture of origin, that is, with generally valued accomplishments. Susan Wolf also emphasizes this:

[17] Will Kymlicka, *Liberalism, Community and Culture* (Oxford: Oxford University Press, 1991).

[18] Cf. R. Forst, *Kontexte der Gerechtigkeit* (Frankfurt am Main: Suhrkamp, forthcoming).

At least one of the serious harms that a failure of recognition perpetuates has little to do with the question of whether the person or the culture who goes unrecognized has anything important to say to all human beings. The need to correct those harms, therefore, does not depend on the presumption or the confirmation of the presumption that a particular culture is distinctively valuable to people outside the culture.[19]

To this extent coexistence with equal rights for different ethnic groups and their cultural forms of life does not need to be safeguarded through the sort of collective rights that would overtax a theory of rights tailored to individual persons. Even if such group rights could be granted in the democratic constitutional state, they would be not only unnecessary but questionable from a normative point of view. For in the last analysis the protection of forms of life and traditions in which identities are formed is supposed to serve the recognition of their members; it does not represent a kind of preservation of species by administrative means. The ecological perspective on species conservation cannot be transferred to cultures. Cultural heritages and the forms of life articulated in them normally reproduce themselves by convincing those whose personality structures they shape, that is, by motivating them to appropriate productively and continue the traditions. The constitutional state can make this hermeneutic achievement of the cultural reproduction of lifeworlds possible, but it cannot guarantee it. For to guarantee survival would necessarily rob the members of the very freedom to say yes or no that is necessary if they are to appropriate and preserve their cultural heritage. When a culture has become reflexive, the only traditions and forms of life that can sustain themselves are those that bind their members while at the same time subjecting themselves to critical examination and leaving later generations the option of learning from other traditions or converting and setting out for

[19] In this volume, p. 79.

other shores. This is true even of relatively closed sects like the Pennsylvania Amish.[20] Even if we considered it a meaningful goal to protect cultures as though they were endangered species, the conditions necessary for them to be able to reproduce successfully would be incompatible with the goal of "maintain[ing] and cherish[ing] distinctness, not just now but forever" (Taylor).

On this point it helps to recall the many subcultures and lifeworlds that flourished in early modern Europe with its occupational stratification, or the forms of life of rural laborers and the deracinated proletarianized urban masses of the first phase of industrialization that succeeded them. Those forms of life were caught up and crushed in the process of modernization, but by no means all of them found their "Meister Anton" and had committed members defending them against the alternatives presented by the new era. And those that were rich and attractive enough to stimulate the will to self-assertion, like the urban culture of the nineteenth century, were able to preserve some of their features only through self-transformation. Even a majority culture that does not consider itself threatened preserves its vitality only through an unrestrained revisionism, by sketching out alternatives to the status quo or by integrating alien impulses— even to the point of breaking with its own traditions. This is especially true of immigrant cultures, which initially define themselves stubbornly in ethnic terms and revive traditional elements under the assimilationist pressure of the new environment, but then quickly develop a mode of life equally distant from both assimilation and tradition.[21]

In multicultural societies the coexistence of forms of life with equal rights means ensuring every citizen the opportunity to grow up within the world of a cultural heritage and to

[20] Cf. the Supreme Court decision in *Wisconsin v. Yoder*, 406 U.S. 205 (1972).

[21] Daniel Cohn-Bendit and Thomas Schmid, *Heimat Babylon* (Hamburg: Hoffmann and Campe, 1992), p. 316ff.

have his or her children grow up in it without suffering discrimination because of it. It means the opportunity to confront this and every other culture and to perpetuate it in its conventional form or transform it; as well as the opportunity to turn away from its commands with indifference or break with it self-critically and then live spurred on by having made a conscious break with tradition, or even with a divided identity. The accelerated pace of change in modern societies explodes all stationary forms of life. Cultures survive only if they draw the strength to transform themselves from criticism and secession. Legal guarantees can be based only on the fact that within his or her own cultural milieu each person retains the possibility of regenerating this strength. And this in turn develops not only by setting oneself apart but at least as much through exchanges with strangers and things alien.

In the modern era rigid forms of life succumb to entropy. Fundamentalist movements can be understood as an ironic attempt to give one's own lifeworld ultrastability by restorative means. The irony lies in the way traditionalism misunderstands itself. In fact, it emerges from the vortex of social modernization and it apes a substance that has already disintegrated. As a reaction to the overwhelming push for modernization, it is itself a thoroughly modern movement of renewal. Nationalism too can turn into fundamentalism, but it should not be confused with it. The nationalism of the French Revolution allied itself with the universalistic principles of the democratic constitutional state; at that time nationalism and republicanism were kindred spirits. On the other hand, fundamentalism afflicts not only societies that are collapsing but even the established democracies of the West. All world religions have produced their own forms of fundamentalism, although by no means all sectarian movements display those traits.

As the Rushdie case reminded us, a fundamentalism that leads to a practice of intolerance is incompatible with the democratic constitutional state. Such a practice is based on religious or historico-philosophical interpretations of the world that claim exclusiveness for a privileged way of life. Such conceptions lack an awareness of the fallibility of their claims, as well as a respect for the "burdens of reason" (Rawls). Of course, religious convictions and global interpretations of the world are not obliged to subscribe to the kind of fallibilism that currently accompanies hypothetical knowledge in the experimental sciences. But fundamentalist worldviews are dogmatic in that they leave no room for reflection on their relationship with the other worldviews with which they share the same universe of discourse and against whose competing validity claims they can advance their positions only on the basis of reasons. They leave no room for "reasonable disagreement."[22]

In contrast, the subjectivized "gods and demons" of the modern world are distinguished by a reflexive attitude that does more than allow for a modus vivendi—something that can be legally enforced given religious freedom. In a spirit of tolerance à la Lessing, the non-fundamentalist worldviews that Rawls characterizes as "not unreasonable comprehensive doctrines"[23] allow for a civilized debate among convictions, in which one party can recognize the other parties as co-combatants in the search for authentic truths without sacrificing its own claims to validity. In multicultural societies the national constitution can tolerate only forms of life articulated within the medium of such non-fundamentalist traditions, because coexistence with equal rights for these forms of life requires the mutual recognition of the different cultural memberships: all persons must also be recognized as members of ethical communities integrated around different conceptions of the good. Hence the ethical integration of

[22] Jürgen Habermas, *Justification and Application: Remarks on Discourse Ethics* (Cambridge, Mass.: MIT Press, 1993).

[23] John Rawls, "The Idea of an Overlapping Consensus," *Oxford Journal of Legal Studies* 7 (1987): 1–25.

groups and subcultures with their own collective identities must be uncoupled from the abstract political integration that includes all citizens equally.

The political integration of citizens ensures loyalty to the common political culture. The latter is rooted in an interpretation of constitutional principles from the perspective of the nation's historical experience. To this extent that interpretation cannot be ethically neutral. Perhaps one would do better to speak of a common horizon of interpretation within which current issues give rise to public debates about the citizens' political self-understanding. The "historians' debate" in 1986–1987 in Germany is a good example of this.[24] But the debates are always about the best interpretation of the same constitutional rights and principles. These form the fixed point of reference for any constitutional patriotism that situates the system of rights within the historical context of a legal community. They must be enduringly linked with the motivations and convictions of the citizens, for without such a motivational anchoring they could not become the driving force behind the dynamically conceived project of producing an association of individuals who are free and equal. Hence the shared political culture in which citizens recognize themselves as members of their polity is also permeated by ethics.

At the same time, the ethical substance of a constitutional patriotism cannot detract from the legal system's neutrality vis-à-vis communities that are ethically integrated at a subpolitical level. Rather, it has to sharpen sensitivity to the diversity and integrity of the different forms of life coexisting within a multicultural society. It is crucial to maintain the distinction between the two levels of integration. If they are collapsed into one another, the majority culture will usurp state prerogatives at the expense of the equal rights of other

---

[24] Jürgen Habermas, *The New Conservatism: Cultural Criticism and the Historians' Debate*, translated by Shierry Weber Nicholsen (Cambridge, Mass.: MIT Press, 1989).

cultural forms of life and violate their claim to mutual recognition. The neutrality of the law vis-à-vis internal ethical differentiations stems from the fact that in complex societies the citizenry as a whole can no longer be held together by a substantive consensus on values but only by a consensus on the procedures for the legitimate enactment of laws and the legitimate exercise of power. Citizens who are politically integrated in this way share the rationally based conviction that unrestrained freedom of communication in the political public sphere, a democratic process for settling conflicts, and the constitutional channeling of political power together provide a basis for checking illegitimate power and ensuring that administrative power is used in the equal interest of all. The universalism of legal principles is reflected in a procedural consensus, which must be embedded in the context of a historically specific political culture through a kind of constitutional patriotism.

IMMIGRATION, CITIZENSHIP AND NATIONAL IDENTITY

Legal experts have the advantage of discussing normative questions in connection with cases to be decided. Their thinking is oriented to application. Philosophers avoid this decisionist pressure; as contemporaries of classical ideas extending over more than two thousand years, they are not embarrassed to consider themselves participants in a conversation that will go on forever. Hence it is all the more fascinating when someone like Charles Taylor attempts to grasp his own times in ideas and to show the relevance of philosophical insights to the pressing political questions of the day. His essay is an example of this, as unusual as it is brilliant—although, or rather because, he does not follow the fashionable path of an "applied ethics."

After the upheavals in Central and Eastern Europe there is another theme on the agenda of the day in Germany and in

135

the European Community as a whole: immigration. After a comprehensive presentation of this problem, a Dutch colleague arrives at the following unadorned prognosis:

> Western European countries ... will do their utmost to prevent immigration from third world countries. To this end they will grant work permits to persons who have skills of immediate relevance to the society in fairly exceptional cases only (soccer players, software specialists from the US, scholars from India, etc.). They will combine a very restrictive entry policy with policies aimed at dealing more quickly and effectively with requests for asylum, and with a practice of deporting without delay those whose request has been denied. ... The conclusion is, that they will individually and jointly use all means at their disposal to stem the tide.[25]

This description fits precisely the compromise on political asylum that the government and the opposition in Germany made the basis for a constitutional change in May 1993. There is no doubt that the great majority of the population welcomes this policy. Xenophobia is widespread these days in the European Community as well. It is more marked in some countries than in others, but the attitudes of the Germans do not differ substantially from those of the French and the English.[26] Taylor's example can encourage us to see how a philosophical point of view can help answer the question of whether this policy of sealing ourselves off from immigration is justified. I will begin by discussing the question in the abstract and then go into the German debate on political asylum and its historical background. I will then outline the alternatives that would have to be discussed in a public debate—one that has not yet taken place—about the ethical-

[25] D. J. van de Kaa, "European Migration at the End of History," *European Review* 1 (January 1993): 94

[26] E. Wiegand, "Ausländerfeindlichkeit in der Festung Europa. Einstellungen zu Fremden im europäischen Vergleich," *Informationsdienst Soziale Indikatoren* (ZUMA), no. 9 (January 1993): 1–4.

political self-understanding of an enlarged Federal Republic of Germany after unification with the German Democratic Republic.

Although modern law is distinguished from post-traditional morality by specific formal characteristics, the system of rights and the principles of the constitutional state are in harmony with morality by virtue of their universalistic content. At the same time, as we have seen, legal systems are "ethically permeated" in that they reflect the political will and the form of life of a specific legal community. The United States, whose political culture is stamped by a constitutional tradition that is two hundred years old, is a good example of this. But the juridified ethos of a nation-state cannot come into conflict with civil rights as long as the political legislature is oriented to constitutional principles and thus to the idea of actualizing basic rights. The ethical substance of a political integration that unites all the citizens of the nation must remain "neutral" with respect to the differences among the ethical-cultural communities within the nation, which are integrated around their own conceptions of the good. The uncoupling of these two levels of integration notwithstanding, a nation of citizens can sustain the institutions of freedom only by developing a certain measure of loyalty to their own state, a loyalty that cannot be legally enforced.

It is this ethical-political self-understanding on the part of the nation that is affected by immigration; for the influx of immigrants alters the composition of the population in ethical-cultural respects as well. Thus the question arises whether the desire for immigration runs up against limits in the right of a political community to maintain its political-cultural form of life intact. Assuming that the autonomously developed state order is indeed shaped by ethics, does the right to self-determination not include the right of a nation to affirm its identity vis-à-vis immigrants who could give a different cast to this historically developed political-cultural form of life?

From the perspective of the recipient society, the problem of immigration raises the question of legitimate conditions of entry. Ignoring the intermediate stages, we can focus on the act of naturalization, with which every state controls the expansion of the political community defined by the rights of citizenship. Under what conditions can the state deny citizenship to those who can advance their claim to naturalization? Aside from the usual provisos (as against criminals), the most relevant question in our context is in what respect a democratic constitutional state can demand that immigrants assimilate in order to maintain the integrity of its citizens' way of life. Philosophically, we can distinguish two levels of assimilation:

(a) assent to the principles of the constitution within the scope of interpretation determined by the ethical-political self-understanding of the citizens and the political culture of the country; in other words, assimilation to the way in which the autonomy of the citizens is institutionalized in the recipient society and the way the "public use of reason" is practiced there;

(b) the further level of a willingness to become acculturated, that is, not only to conform externally but to become habituated to the way of life, the practices, and customs of the local culture. This means an assimilation that penetrates to the level of ethical-cultural integration and thereby has a deeper impact on the collective identity of the immigrants' culture of origin than the political socialization required under (a) above.

The results of the immigration policy practiced in the United States support a liberal interpretation that exemplifies the first of these alternatives.[27] An example of the second is the Prussian policy on immigration from Poland under Bis-

[27] Michael Walzer, "What Does It Mean to Be an American?" *Social Research* 57 (Fall 1990): 591–614. Walzer notes that the communitarian conception does not take account of the complex composition of a multicultural society (p. 613).

marck, which despite variations was oriented primarily to Germanization.[28]

A democratic constitutional state that is serious about uncoupling these two levels of integration can require of immigrants only the political socialization described in (a) above (and practically speaking can expect to see it only in the second generation). This enables it to preserve the identity of the political community, which nothing, including immigration, can be permitted to encroach upon, since that identity is founded on the constitutional principles anchored in the political culture and not on the basic ethical orientations of the cultural form of life predominant in that country. Accordingly, all that needs to be expected of immigrants is the willingness to enter into the political culture of their new homeland, without having to give up the cultural form of life of their origins by doing so. The right to democratic self-determination does indeed include the right of citizens to insist on the inclusive character of their own political culture; it safeguards the society from the danger of segmentation—from the exclusion of alien subcultures and from a separatist disintegration into unrelated subcultures. As I indicated above, political integration also excludes fundamentalist immigrant cultures. Aside from this, it does not justify compulsory assimilation for the sake of the self-affirmation of the cultural form of life dominant in the country.[29]

This constitutional alternative has an important implication, however, namely, that the legitimately asserted identity of the political community will by no means be preserved from alterations in the long run in the wake of waves of immigration. Because immigrants cannot be compelled to surrender their own traditions, as other forms of life become established the horizon within which citizens henceforth

[28] Roger Brubaker, *Citizenship and Nationhood in France and Germany* (Cambridge, Mass.: Harvard University Press, 1992), p. 128ff.

[29] Cohn-Bendit and Schmid, *Heimat Babylon*, chap. 8.

interpret their common constitutional principles may also expand. Then the mechanism comes into play whereby a change in the composition of the active citizenry changes the context to which the ethical-political self-understanding of the nation as a whole refers: "People live in communities with bonds and bounds, but these may be of different kinds. In a liberal society, the bonds and bounds should be compatible with liberal principles. Open immigration would change the character of the community, but it would not leave the community without any character."[30]

Let me now turn from the question of the conditions a democratic constitutional state may impose on the reception of immigrants to another question: Who has the right to immigrate?

There are good moral grounds for an individual legal right to political asylum (in the sense of Article 16 of the German Basic Law [*Grundgesetz*], which must be interpreted with reference to the protection of human dignity guaranteed in Article 1 and in connection with the guarantee of legal recourse established in Article 19). I do not need to go into them here. What is important is the definition of a refugee. In accordance with Article 13 of the Geneva Convention on the Status of Refugees, someone is considered to be entitled to asylum if he is fleeing from a country "where his life or freedom would be threatened on account of his race, religion, nationality, membership of a particular social group or political opinion." In the light of recent experience this definition needs to be extended to include the protection of women from mass rapes. The right to temporary asylum for refugees from civil war regions is also unproblematic. But since the discovery of America, and especially since the explosive increase in worldwide immigration in the eighteenth century,

---

[30] J. H. Carens, "Aliens and Citizens," *Review of Politics* 49 (1987): 271; cf. also Jürgen Habermas, "Staatsbürgerschaft und nationale Identität," in Habermas, *Faktizität und Geltung*, pp. 632–60. An earlier version of this essay appeared in English as "Citizenship and National Identity," *Praxis International* 12 (1992): 1–19.

the great bulk of those wanting to immigrate has consisted of individuals immigrating in order to work and refugees from poverty who want to escape a miserable existence in their homeland. And so it is today. It is against this immigration from the impoverished regions of the East and the South that a European chauvinism of affluence is now arming itself.

One can cite good grounds for a moral claim. People do not normally leave their homelands except under dire circumstances; as a rule the mere fact that they have fled is sufficient evidence of their need for help. In particular, an obligation to provide assistance arises from the growing interdependencies of a global society that has become so enmeshed through the capitalist world market and electronic mass communications that the United Nations has assumed something like an overall political responsibility for safeguarding life on the planet, as the recent example of Somalia indicates. Further, special duties are devolved upon the First World as a result of the history of colonization and the uprooting of regional cultures by the incursion of capitalist modernization. We should also note that in the period between 1800 and 1960 Europeans were disproportionately represented in intercontinental migratory movements, making up 80 percent of those involved, and they profited from this—that is, they improved their living conditions in comparison with other migrants and with those of their compatriots who did not emigrate. At the same time, the exodus of the nineteenth and early twentieth centuries improved the economic situations in the countries from which they fled, just as decisively as did, conversely, the immigration to Europe during the reconstruction period following the Second World War.[31] Either way, Europe was the beneficiary of these streams of migration.

From the moral point of view we cannot regard this problem solely from the perspective of the inhabitants of

---

[31] P. C. Emmer, "Intercontinental Migration," *European Review* 1 (January 1993): 67–74: "After 1800 the dramatic increase in the economic growth

affluent and peaceful societies; we must also take the perspective of those who come to foreign continents seeking their well-being, that is, an existence worthy of human beings, rather than protection from political persecution. The question of a legal claim to immigration is particularly relevant in the current situation, where the number of people wanting to immigrate manifestly exceeds the willingness to receive them.

These and other related moral reasons that could be given do not, to be sure, justify guaranteeing actionable individual legal rights to immigration but they do justify an obligation to have a liberal immigration policy that opens one's own society to immigrants and regulates the flow of immigration in relation to existing capacities. In the defensive slogan "the boat is full" one hears a lack of willingness to take the perspective of the other side—of the "boat people" in their shaky craft, for example, trying to escape the terror in Indochina. European societies, shrinking demographically and dependent on immigration if only for economic reasons, have certainly not reached the limits of their capacity to absorb immigrants. The moral basis for a liberal immigration policy also gives rise to an obligation not to limit immigration quotas to the recipient country's economic needs, that is, to "welcome technical expertise," but instead to establish quotas in accordance with criteria that are acceptable from the perspective of all parties involved.

---

of Western Europe could only be maintained as an 'escape hatch.' The escape of 61 million Europeans after 1800 allowed the European economies to create such a mix of the factors of production as to allow for record economic growth and to avoid a situation in which economic growth was absorbed by an increase in population. After the Second World War, Europeans also benefitted from intercontinental migration since the colonial empires forced many colonial subjects to migrate to the metropolis. In this particular period there was no danger of overpopulation. . . . Many of the colonial migrants coming to Europe had been well trained and they arrived at exactly the time when skilled labour was at a premium in rebuilding Europe's economy." (p. 72f.)

The Politics of Asylum in a United Germany

If one takes these principles as a point of departure, the compromise on political asylum negotiated between the German government and the opposition Social Democrats cannot be justified in normative terms. Without going into detail, I will list the three central flaws of the agreement and criticize the premises on which they are based.

The regulations provided for by the agreement are limited to political asylum, that is, to measures directed against "abuses" of the right to asylum. They ignore the fact that Germany needs an immigration policy that provides immigrants with other legal options as well. The problem of immigration is falsely defined in a way that has numerous implications. Anyone who dissolves the connection between the question of political asylum and the question of immigration in flight from poverty is implicitly declaring that he or she wants to evade Europe's moral obligation to refugees from the impoverished regions of the world and is willing to tolerate instead a flow of illegal and uncontrollable immigration that can always be labelled "abuse of asylum" and used for domestic political purposes.

The addition of an Article 16a to the Basic Law weakens the substance of the individual legal right to political asylum because it allows refugees coming into the country from a so-called "safe third country" to be deported without legal recourse. This shifts the burden of immigration to Eastern Europe, to our neighbors Poland, the Czech Republic, Slovakia, Hungary, and Austria—in other words, to countries that are currently ill prepared to handle this problem in a legally unobjectionable way. In addition, curtailing the guarantee of legal protection for refugees from countries defined as "free of persecution" from Germany's point of view is problematic.

Rather than making it easier for foreigners already residing in Germany, especially the *Gastarbeiter* [literally, guest

143

workers] whom we recruited, to acquire citizenship, the asylum compromise left the naturalization laws unchanged. The dual citizenship that those foreigners understandably prefer is denied them; even children born to them in Germany do not automatically receive the rights of citizenship. Foreigners who are willing to renounce their previous citizenship can be naturalized only after they have been living in Germany for at least fifteen years. In contrast, the so-called *Volksdeutschen* or ethnic Germans—primarily Poles and Russians who can prove German ancestry—have a constitutional right to naturalization. In 1992, in addition to approximately 500,000 asylum seekers (of which 130,000 were from the civil war regions of the former Yugloslavia), 220,000 ethnic-German immigrants were accepted into Germany on this basis.

The German policy on political asylum rests on the repeatedly reaffirmed premise that Germany is not a land of immigration. This contradicts not only what we all see in the streets and subways of our metropolises—today 26 percent of the population of Frankfurt consists of foreigners—but also the historical facts. To be sure, since the early nineteenth century almost 8 million Germans have emigrated to the United States alone. But at the same time, major waves of immigration have occurred during the last hundred years. By the First World War 1.2 million immigrant workers had entered the country, and 12 million "displaced persons" were left behind at the end of the Second World War—primarily forced labor deported from Poland and the Soviet Union. In 1955, following the path laid out by the Nazi policy of forced foreign labor, and despite relatively high unemployment in Germany, came the organized recruiting of a cheap, unmarried male workforce from the south and from Southeastern Europe. This continued until recruitment ceased in 1973. Today the families and offspring of those *Gastarbeiter* who did not return to their own countries live in the paradoxical situation of immigrants with no clear prospects for immigration—Germans with foreign passports.[32] They form the bulk of the 8.2 percent of the 1990 German population composed of foreigners living in Germany. Without them an economic boom now comparable only to that of Japan would not have been possible, and it is even harder to understand the resistance to the full integration of these foreigners when one considers that by 1990 West Germany had integrated 15 million refugees, immigrants, and foreigners who were either German or of German descent—thus also *Neubürger*, new citizens: "If a foreign population of about 4.8 million is added, nearly one-third of the West-German population has resulted from immigration movements since World War II."[33]

If the notion that "we are not a land of immigration" continues to be put forth in the political public sphere in the face of this evidence, this indicates that it is a manifestation of a deep-seated mentality—and that a painful change is necessary in the way we conceive ourselves as a nation. It is no accident that our naturalization decisions are based on the principle of ancestry and not, as in other Western nations, on the principle of territoriality. The shortcomings described above in the way Germany is dealing with the problem of immigration must be understood against the historical background of the Germans' understanding of themselves as a nation of *Volksgenossen* or ethnic comrades centered around language and culture. Anyone who is born in France is considered to be French and holds the rights of a French citizen. In Germany, until the end of the Second World War fine distinctions were still being made between *Deutschen*, or citizens of German descent; *Reichsdeutschen*, or German citizens of non-German descent; and *Volksdeutschen*, or individuals of German descent living in other countries.

---

[32] K. J. Bade, "Immigration and Integration in Germany since 1945," *European Review* 1 (January 1993): 75–79.

[33] Bade, p. 77.

In France national consciousness could develop within the framework of a territorial state, while in Germany it was originally linked with the romantically inspired educated middle-class notion of a *Kulturnation*, a nation defined by its culture. This idea represented an imaginary unity that had to seek support in a shared language, tradition, and ancestry in order to transcend the reality of the existing small states in Germany. Still more important was the fact that the French national consciousness could develop in step with the establishment of democratic civil liberties and in the struggle against the sovereignty of the French king, whereas German nationalism arose out of the struggle against Napoleon, thus against an external enemy, independently of the battle for democratic civil liberties and long before the *kleindeutsche* nation state was imposed from above. Having emerged from a "war of liberation" of this kind, national consciousness in Germany could be linked with the pathos of the uniqueness of its culture and ancestry—a particularism that has enduringly stamped the Germans' self-understanding.

The Federal Republic of Germany turned away from this *Sonderbewusstsein* or sense of specialness after 1945, after the shock of the collapse of civilization in the Nazi mass exterminations, a shock it only gradually came to terms with. Loss of sovereignty and a marginal position in a polarized world reinforced this. Reunification and the dissolution of the Soviet Union have changed this constellation in a fundamental way. Hence the reactions to the right-wing radicalism that has flared up again—and in this context the deceptive debate on asylum as well—raise the question whether the enlarged Federal Republic will continue on its path toward a more clvilized politics or whether the old *Sonderbewusstsein* is being regenerated in a different form. This question is complicated by the fact that the process of national unification was pushed through and administratively manipulated from above and has set a false course for the country in this respect as well. Discussion and clarification of the ethical-political self-understanding of the citizens of two German states with widely divergent historical fates is urgently needed but has not yet taken place. The "accession" of new *Länder*, or federal states—a constitutionally dubious legal option—prevented a constitutional debate, and positions in the debate about the seat of the German capital are skewed. In the meantime the citizens of the former East Germany, humiliated in many ways and deprived of their spokespersons and a political public sphere of their own, have other problems to contend with; in place of clearly articulated contributions to the debate they find smoldering resentments.

All repression produces symptoms. One challenge after another—from the Gulf War to Maastrich, the civil war in Yugoslavia, the asylum issue and right-wing radicalism, to the deployment of German military forces outside the NATO area—arouse a sense of helplessness in the political public sphere and in an immobilized government. The changed constellation of power and a changed domestic situation certainly demand new responses. The question is, with what kind of consciousness will Germany make the adaptations required if it continues its pattern of reacting with ad hoc decisions and subliminal mood shifts?

Historians who dash off books with titles like "Back to History" and "Fear of Power" offer us a backward-looking farewell to the old Federal Republic that purports to expose the recently celebrated success story of postwar German democracy as a *Sonderweg* or special path of its own. The former West Germany is said to have embodied the forced abnormality of a defeated and divided nation, and now, having recovered its national greatness and sovereignty, it must be led out of its utopianism, with its obliviousness to power, and back to the path of self-conscious preeminence in Central Europe, the path of power politics marked out by Bismarck. This celebration of the caesura of 1989 hides the repeatedly frustrated desire for normalization of those who did not want to accept the caesura of 1945. They reject an alternative that does not necessarily lead to other options at every turn in the short run but instead opens up another perspective by understanding the leavetaking from the old Federal Republic differently. In this alternative view, West Germany's orientation to the West represents not a shrewd but episodic foreign policy decision, and above all not solely a political decision, but rather a profound intellectual break with those specifically German traditions that stamped the Wilhelminian Empire and contributed to the downfall of the Weimar Republic. That break set the stage for a shift in mentality that affected broad segments of the public after the youth revolt of 1968 and under the favorable conditions of an affluent society, a shift that made it possible for democracy and the constitutional state to take political and cultural root in German soil for the first time. Today what is at stake is adapting Germany's political role to new realities, without letting the process of civilizing politics that was underway until 1989 be broken off under the pressure of the economic and social problems of unification, and without sacrificing the normative achievements of a national self-understanding that is no longer based on ethnicity but founded on citizenship.

Identity, Authenticity, Survival

MULTICULTURAL SOCIETIES AND

SOCIAL REPRODUCTION

K. ANTHONY APPIAH

I

C HARLES TAYLOR is surely right that much of modern social and political life turns on questions of recognition. In our liberal tradition we see recognition largely as a matter of acknowledging individuals and what we call their identities. We also have the notion, which comes (as Taylor also rightly says) from the ethics of authenticity, that, other things being equal, people have the right to be acknowledged publicly as what they already really are. It is because someone is already authentically Jewish or gay that we deny them something in requiring them to hide this fact, to pass for something that they are not.

As has often been pointed out, however, the way much discussion of recognition proceeds is strangely at odds with the individualist thrust of talk of authenticity and identity. If what matters about me is my individual and authentic self, why is so much contemporary talk of identity about large categories—gender, ethnicity, nationality, "race,"[1] sexuality—that seem so far from individual? What is the relation

---

[1] I have spent enough time arguing against the reality of "races" to feel unhappy about using the term without scare quotes. See *In My Father's House: Africa in the Philosophy of Culture* (New York: Oxford University Press, 1992), *passim*.

between this collective language and the individualist thrust
of the modern notion of the self? How has social life come to
be so bound up with an idea of identity that has deep roots
in Romanticism, with its celebration of the individual over
society?[2]

One strand of Taylor's rich essay is a cogent defense of a
set of answers to these questions. I discuss here some features of his story under the rubrics of identity, authenticity,
and survival. In essence, I want to take up some complica-
tions about each of these three crucial terms.

II

Identity

In the course of my life I have seen Frenchmen, Italians,
Russians; I even know, thanks to Montesquieu, that one
can be a Persian; but *man* I have never met.
Joseph de Maistre[3]

The identities whose recognition Taylor discusses are largely
what we can call collective social identities: religion, gender,
ethnicity, "race," sexuality. This list is somewhat heterogeneous; such collective identities matter to their bearers and
to others in very different ways. Religion, for example, unlike all the others, entails attachments to creeds or commitment to practices. Gender and sexuality, unlike the rest, are
both grounded in the sexual body; both are differently expe-
rienced at different places and times. Still, everywhere that I

---

[2] Taylor reminds us rightly of Trilling's profound contributions to our
understanding of this history. I discuss Trilling's work in chapter 4 of *In
My Father's House*.

[3] Joseph de Maistre, *Considérations sur la France* (2d ed. London; Bâle,
1797), p. 102. "J'ai vu, dans ma vie, des Francis, des Italiens, des Russes,
etc.; je sais même, graces à Montesquieu, qu'on peut être Persan: mais
quant à l'homme, je déclare ne l'avoir recontré de ma vie. . . ."

know of, gender identity proposes norms of behavior, dress, and character. Of course, gender and sexuality are, despite these abstract similarities, in many ways profoundly different. In our society, for example, passing as a woman or a man is hard, while passing as straight (or gay) is relatively easy. There are other collective identities—disabled people, for example—that have sought recognition, modeling themselves sometimes on racial minorities (with whom they share the experience of discrimination and insult), or (as with deaf people) on ethnic groups. And there are castes, in South Asia, clans on every continent, and classes, with enormously varying degrees of class consciousness, all over the industrialized world. But the major collective identities that demand recognition in North America currently are religion, gender, ethnicity, "race," and sexuality.[4] That they matter to us for reasons so heterogeneous should, I think, make us careful not to assume that what goes for one goes for the others.

The connection between individual identity, on the one hand, which is the focus of Taylor's discussion, and these collective identities, on the other, seems to be something like this: Each person's individual identity is seen as having two major dimensions. There is a collective dimension, the intersection of their collective identities, and there is a personal dimension, consisting of other socially or morally important features—intelligence, charm, wit, cupidity—that are not themselves the basis of forms of collective identity.

The distinction between these two dimensions of identity is, so to speak, a sociological rather than a logical distinction. In each dimension we are talking about properties that are important for social life, but only the collective identities count as social categories, as kinds of persons. There is a logical but no social category of the witty, or the clever, or the

[4] In the United States we deal with what Herder would have recognized as national differences (differences, in Taylor's formulation, between one society and another within the American nation) through concepts of ethnicity.

151

charming, or the greedy. People who share these properties do not constitute a social group, in the relevant sense.

I shall return to the question of why these particular properties constitute the bases for social categories that demand recognition; for the moment, I shall rely on an intuitive grasp of the distinction between the personal and the collective dimensions of individual identity. I turn now to "authenticity" in order to bring out something important about the connection between these two dimensions.

III

Authenticity

> The artist—as he comes to be called—ceases to be the craftsman or the performer, dependent upon the approval of the audience. His reference is to himself only, or to some transcendent power which—or who—has decreed his enterprise and alone is worthy to judge it.
> *Lionel Trilling*[5]

Taylor is right to remind us of Trilling's brilliant discussion of the modern self, and, more particularly, of the ideal of authenticity. Taylor captures that idea in a few elegant sentences: "There is a certain way of being that is *my* way. I am called upon to live my life in this way. . . . If I am not [true to myself], I miss the point of my life" (p. 30).

Trilling's theme is the expression of this idea in literature and in our understanding of the role of the artist as the archetype of the authentic person. If there is one part of Trilling's picture that Taylor leaves out, it is that for Romanticism the search for authenticity is demonstrated at least as much in opposition to the demands of social life as it is in the rec-

---

[5] Lionel Trilling, *Sincerity and Authenticity* (Cambridge, Mass.: Harvard University Press, 1971), p. 97.

ognition of one's own real self. In the precisely titled collection, *The Opposing Self*, Trilling writes of *The Scholar Gypsy* (as the model of the artist) that "his existence is intended to disturb us and make us dissatisfied with our habitual life in culture."[6]

Taylor's topic is the politics of recognition; attending to the oppositional aspects of authenticity would complicate the picture, because it would bring sharply into focus the difference between two levels of authenticity that the contemporary politics of recognition seems to conflate. To elicit the problem, let me start with a point Taylor makes in passing about Herder:

> I should note here that Herder applied his conception of originality at two levels, not only to the individual person among other persons, but also to the culture-bearing people among other peoples. Just like individuals, a *Volk* should be true to itself, that is, its own culture (p. 31).

This way of framing the issue does not pay enough attention to the connection between the originality of persons and of nations. After all, in many places nowadays the individual identity, whose putative authenticity screams out for recognition, is likely to have what Herder would have seen as a national identity as a component of its collective dimension. My being, say, an African-American among other things, shapes the authentic self that I seek to express.[7] And it is, in part, because I seek to express my self that I seek recognition of an African-American identity. This is the fact that makes problems for Trilling's opposing self, for recognition as an African-American means social acknowledgment of that collective identity, which requires not just recognizing its existence but actually demonstrating respect for it. If, in understanding myself as African-American, I see myself as resist-

[6] Lionel Trilling, *The Opposing Self: Nine Essays in Criticism* (New York: Viking Press, 1955), p. xiv.

[7] For Herder, this would be a paradigmatic national identity.

ing white norms, mainstream American conventions, the racism (and, perhaps, the materialism or the individualism) of "white culture," why should I at the same time seek recognition from these white others?

There is, in other words, at least an irony in the way in which an ideal—I could call it the Bohemian ideal—in which authenticity requires us to reject much that is conventional in our society is turned around and made the basis of a "politics of recognition." Irony is not the Bohemian's only problem. It seems to me that this notion of authenticity has built into it a series of errors of philosophical anthropology. It is, first of all, wrong in failing to see what Taylor so clearly recognizes: the way in which the self is, as he says, dialogically constituted. The rhetoric of authenticity proposes not only that I have a way of being that is all my own, but that in developing it I must fight against the family, organized religion, society, the school, the state—all the forces of convention. This is wrong, however, not only because it is in dialogue with other people's understandings of who I am that I develop a conception of my own identity (Taylor's point) but also because my identity is crucially constituted through concepts and practices made available to me by religion, society, school, and state, and mediated to varying degrees by the family. Dialogue shapes the identity I develop as I grow up, but the very material out of which I form it is provided, in part, by my society, by what Taylor calls its language in "a broad sense."[8] Taylor's term "monological" can be extended to describe views of authenticity that make these connected errors.

Not all will find these insights palatable. A black nationalist might state her case this way: "African-American identity is shaped by African-American society, culture, and religion. It is dialogue with these black others that shapes the black

[8] The broad sense "cover[s] not only the words we speak, but also other modes of expression whereby we define ourselves, including the 'languages' of art, of gesture, of love, and the like" (p. 32).

self; it is from these black contexts that the concepts through which African-Americans shape themselves are derived. The white society, the white culture, against which an African-American nationalism of the counterconventional kind poses itself, is therefore not part of what shapes the collective dimension of the individual identities of black people in the United States."

This claim seems to me to be simply false. After all, it is in part a recognition of a black identity by "white society" that is demanded by nationalism of this form. And "recognition" here means what Taylor means by it, not mere acknowledgment of existence. African-American identity is centrally shaped by American society and institutions; it cannot be seen as constructed solely within African-American communities.

There is, I think, another error in the standard framing of authenticity as an ideal, and that is the philosophical realism (which is nowadays usually called "essentialism") that seems inherent in the way questions of authenticity are normally posed. Authenticity speaks of the real self buried in there, the self one has to dig out and express. It is only later, in reaction to Romanticism, that the idea develops that a self is something that one creates, makes up, so that every life should be an art work whose creator is, in some sense, his or her own greatest creation. (This is an idea one of whose sources, I suppose, is Oscar Wilde.)

Of course, neither the picture in which there is just an authentic nugget of selfhood, the core that is distinctively me, waiting to be dug out, nor the notion that I can simply make up any self I choose, should tempt us. We make up selves from a tool kit of options made available by our culture and society. We do make choices, but we do not determine the options among which we choose.[9] This raises the question of how much we should acknowledge authenticity in our politi-

[9] This is too simple as well, for reasons captured in Anthony Giddens's many discussions of "duality of structure." See Giddens, *Central Problems in Social Theory* (Berkeley: University of California Press, 1979); and *The Constitution of Society* (Cambridge: Polity Press, 1984).

cal morality, and that depends on whether an account of it can be developed that is neither essentialist nor monological.

It would be too large a claim that the identities that claim recognition in the multicultural chorus *must* be essentialist and monological. But it seems to me that one reasonable ground for suspicion of much contemporary multicultural talk is that it presupposes conceptions of collective identity that are remarkably unsubtle in their understandings of the processes by which identities, both individual and collective, develop. I am not sure whether Taylor would agree with me that collective identities disciplined by historical knowledge and philosophical reflection would be radically unlike the identities that now parade before us for recognition and would raise, as a result, questions different from those he addresses.

In a rather unphilosophical nutshell, my suspicion is that Taylor is happier with the collective identities that actually inhabit our globe than I am, and that may be one of the reasons why I am less disposed to make the concessions to them that he does. These differences in sympathy show up in the area of group survival, to which I now turn.

IV

Survival

Policies aimed at survival actively seek to create
members of the community, for instance, in their
assuring that future generations continue to
identify as French-speakers.
Charles Taylor (pp. 58–59)

Taylor argues that the reality of plural societies may require us to modify procedural liberalism. I think he is right in thinking that there is not much to be said for the view that liberalism should be purely procedural. I agree that we should not accept both (a) the insistence on the uniform application of rules without exception and (b) the suspicion of collective goals (p. 60); I agree that the reason we cannot accept (a) is that we should reject (b) (p. 61). There can be legitimate collective goals whose pursuit will require giving up pure proceduralism.

But Taylor's argument for collective goals in the vast majority of modern states, which are multicultural, is that one very strong demand, to which the state may need to accede, may be for the survival of certain "societies," by which he means groups whose continuity through time consists in the transmission through the generations of a certain culture, of distinctive institutions, values, and practices. And he claims (p. 41n) that the desire for survival is not simply the desire that the culture that gives meaning to the lives of currently existing individuals should continue for them, but requires the continued existence of the culture through indefinite future generations.

I would like to suggest a focus different from Taylor's in his discussion of this issue. Let me stress first that the indefinite future generations in question should be the descendants of the current population. The desire for the survival of French Canadian identity is not the desire that there should always be people somewhere who speak that Quebec language and practice those Quebec practices. It is the desire that this language and practice should be carried on from one generation to the next. A proposal to solve the problems of Canada by paying a group of unrelated people to carry on French Canadian culture on some island in the South Pacific simply would not meet the need.

This matters because it seems to me not at all clear that this aim is one that we can acknowledge while respecting the autonomy of future individuals. In particular families it is often the case that parents want the children to persist in some practice that those children resist. This is true for arranged marriage for some women of Indian origin in Britain, for example. In this case, the ethical principles of equal dignity that underlie liberal thinking seem to militate against allowing the parents their way because we care about the autonomy of these young women. If this is true in the individual case, it seems to me equally true where a whole generation of one group wishes to impose a form of life on the next generation—and a fortiori true if they seek to impose it somehow on still later generations.

Of course, speaking abstractly, survival is perfectly consistent in this sense with respect for autonomy, otherwise every genuinely liberal society would have to die in a generation. If we create a culture that our descendants will want to hold on to, our culture will survive in them. But here there is a deep problem that has to do with the question of how a respect for autonomy should constrain our ethics of education. After all, we have it in our power to some extent to make our children into the kind of people who will want to maintain our culture. Precisely because the monological view of identity is incorrect, there is no individual nugget waiting in each child to express itself, if only family and society permit its unfettered development. We have to help children make themselves, and we have to do so according to our values because children do not begin with values of their own. To value autonomy is to respect the conceptions of others, to weigh their plans for themselves very heavily in deciding what is good for them, even though children do not start out with plans or conceptions. It follows, therefore, in education in the broad sense—the sense that is covered by the technical notion of social reproduction—we simply must both appeal to and transmit values more substantial than a respect for liberal procedures. Liberal proceduralism is meant to allow a state to be indifferent among a variety of conceptions of the good, but this variety itself will depend on what goes on in education. Teach all children only that they must accept a politics in which other people's conceptions of the good are not ridden over and we risk a situation in which there are substantive conceptions of the good incompatible with liberal principle or, at least, with each other. This is the point that Taylor adverts to in pointing to the problem raised by the Rushdie affair. This is why liberalism must, in the end, be ready to be a fighting creed.

In most modern societies, the education of most people is conducted by institutions run by the government. Education is, therefore, in the political domain. This is not just an accident: social reproduction involves collective goals. Furthermore, as children develop and come to have identities whose autonomy we should respect, the liberal state has a role in protecting the autonomy of children against their parents, churches, and communities. I would be prepared to defend the view that the state in modern society must be involved in education on this sort of basis, but even if someone disagrees with this they must admit that it does play such a role currently and that this means that the state is involved in propagating elements, at least, of a substantive conception of the good.

That is one of the major reasons why I agree so wholeheartedly with Taylor's objections to pure proceduralism. I do not think that it is Taylor's reason, however, even though he does raise his objections to pure proceduralism in the context of a discussion of survival—that is, of social reproduction.

V

The large collective identities that call for recognition come with notions of how a proper person of that kind behaves: it is not that there is *one* way that gays or blacks should behave, but that there are gay and black modes of behavior. These notions provide loose norms or models, which play a role in shaping the life plans of those who make these collective identities central to their individual identities.[10] Collective

---

[10] I say "make," here, not because I think there is always conscious attention to the shaping of life plans or a substantial experience of choice, but because I want to stress the antiessentialist point that there are choices that can be made.

identities, in short, provide what we might call scripts: narratives that people can use in shaping their life plans and in
telling their life stories. In our society (though not, perhaps,
in the England of Addison and Steele) being witty does not
in this way suggest the life-script of "the wit." And that is
why the personal dimensions of identity work differently
from the collective ones.[11]

This is not just a point about modern Westerners: crosscul-
turally it matters to people that their lives have a certain narrative unity; they want to be able to tell a story of their lives
that makes sense. The story—my story—should cohere in
the way appropriate by the standards made available in my
culture to a person of my identity. In telling that story, how
I fit into the wider story of various collectivities is, for most
of us, important. It is not just gender identities that give
shape (through, for example, rites of passage into woman- or
manhood) to one's life: ethnic and national identities too fit
each individual story into a larger narrative. And some of the
most individualist of individuals value such things. Hobbes
spoke of the desire for glory as one of the dominating impulses of human beings, one that was bound to make trouble
for social life. But glory can consist in fitting and being seen
to fit into a collective history, and so, in the name of glory,
one can end up doing the most social things of all.

In our current situation in the multicultural West, we live
in societies in which certain individuals have not been

---

[11] There are other identities that come with scripts, so it will not do to
distinguish just the small class of collective identities from the personal
ones that do not. "Intellectual," "artist," professional identities like
"teacher," "lawyer," "politician" all differ from the large collective identities I have been discussing in a couple of ways that I would point to in
developing a further account: they tend not to depend in the same way on
properties (like ancestry and the sexual body) that are (conceived of as)
not optional; and they tend not to be central to childhood, intergenera-
tional relations, and family life. There are few sharp distinctions in this
area. The point of the analytic distinction between scripted and unscripted
identities is to explore an issue, not to provide the beginnings of a set of
rigid categories.

treated with equal dignity because they were, for example, women, homosexuals, blacks, Catholics. Because, as Taylor so persuasively argues, our identities are dialogically shaped, people who have these characteristics find them central—often negatively so—to their identities. Nowadays there is a widespread agreement that the insults to their dignity and the limitations of their autonomy imposed in the name of these collective identities are seriously wrong. One form of healing the self that those who have these identities participate in is learning to see these collective identities not as sources of limitation and insult but as a valuable part of what they centrally are. Because the ethics of authenticity requires us to express what we centrally are, they further demand recognition in social life as women, homosexuals, blacks, Catholics. Because there was no good reason to treat people of these sorts badly, and because the culture continues to provide degrading images of them nevertheless, they demand that we do cultural work to resist the stereotypes, to challenge the insults, to lift the restrictions.

These old restrictions suggested life-scripts for the bearers of these identities, but they were negative ones. In order to construct a life with dignity, it seems natural to take the collective identity and construct positive life-scripts instead. An African-American after the Black Power movement takes the old script of self-hatred, the script in which he or she is a nigger, and works, in community with others, to construct a series of positive Black life-scripts. In these life-scripts, being a Negro is recoded as being Black, and this requires, among other things, refusing to assimilate to white norms of speech and behavior. And if one is to be Black in a society that is racist then one has to deal constantly with assaults on one's dignity. In this context, insisting on the right to live a dignified life will not be enough. It will not even be enough to require being treated with equal dignity despite being Black, for that will require a concession that being Black counts naturally or to some degree against one's dignity. And so one will end up asking to be respected *as a Black*.

The same example holds for gay identity. An American homosexual after Stonewall and gay liberation takes the old script of self-hatred, the script of the closet, the script in which he is a faggot, and works, in community with others, to construct a series of positive gay life-scripts. In these life-scripts, being homosexual, is recoded as being gay, and this requires, among other things, refusing to stay in the closet. And if one is to be out of the closet in a society that deprives homosexuals of equal dignity and respect then one has to deal constantly with assaults on one's dignity. In this context, the right to live as an "open homosexual" will not be enough. It will not even be enough to be treated with equal dignity despite being homosexual, for that will require a concession that being homosexual counts naturally or to some degree against one's dignity. And so one will end up asking to be respected *as a homosexual*.

This is the sort of story Taylor tells, with sympathy, about Quebec. I am sympathetic to the stories of gay and black identity I have just told. I see how the story goes. It may even be historically, strategically necessary for the story to go this way.[12] But I think we need to go on to the next necessary step, which is to ask whether the identities constructed in this way are ones we—I speak here as someone who counts in America as a gay black man—can be happy with in the longer run. Demanding respect for people as blacks and as gays requires that there are some scripts that go with being an African-American or having same-sex desires. There will be proper ways of being black and gay, there will be expectations to be met, demands will be made. It is at this point that someone who takes autonomy seriously will ask whether we

---

[12] Compare what Sartre wrote in his "Orphée Noir" in *Anthologie de la Nouvelle Poésie Nègre et Malagache de Langue Francaise* (ed. L. S. Senghor), p. xiv. Sartre argued, in effect, that this move is a necessary step in a dialectical progression. In this passage he explicitly argues that what he calls an "antiracist racism" is a path to the "final unity . . . the abolition of differences of race."

have not replaced one kind of tyranny with another. If I had to choose between the world of the closet and the world of gay liberation, or between the world of *Uncle Tom's Cabin* and Black Power, I would, of course, choose in each case the latter. But I would like not to have to choose. I would like other options. The politics of recognition requires that one's skin color, one's sexual body, should be acknowledged politically in ways that make it hard for those who want to treat their skin and their sexual body as personal dimensions of the self. And personal means not secret, but not too tightly scripted. I think (and Taylor, I gather, does not) that the desire of some Quebecois to require people who are "ethnically" francophone to teach their children in French steps over a boundary. I believe (to pronounce on a topic Taylor does not address) that this is, in some sense, the same boundary that is crossed by someone who demands that I organize my life around my "race" or my sexuality.

It is a familiar thought that the bureaucratic categories of identity must come up short before the vagaries of actual people's lives. But it is equally important to bear in mind that a politics of identity can be counted on to transform the identities on whose behalf it ostensibly labors.[13] Between the politics of recognition and the politics of compulsion, there is no bright line.

[13] This is another point essentialists are ill equipped to see.

❖ Contributors ❖

KWAME ANTHONY APPIAH is Professor of Afro-American Studies and Philosophy at Harvard University. He was raised in Ghana and educated at Cambridge University, where he received both his B.A. and his Ph.D. in philosophy. His many books include *Assertion and Conditionals*, *For Truth in Semantics*, *Necessary Questions*, and *In My Father's House*. He is also the author of two mystery novels, *Avenging Angel* and *Nobody Likes Letitia*. Professor Appiah's scholarly interests range over African and African-American intellectual history and literary studies, ethics, and philosophy of mind and language; he has also taught regularly on philosophical problems in the study of African traditional religions. He has been Chairman of the Joint Committee on African Studies of the Social Science Research Council and the American Council of Learned Societies and President of the Society for African Philosophy in North America. He is an editor of *Transition* magazine, and has taught at Cambridge, Yale, Cornell, Duke, and at the University of Ghana.

AMY GUTMANN is Laurance S. Rockefeller University Professor of Politics at Princeton University and the Director of the University Center for Human Values and the Program in Ethics and Public Affairs. Among her publications are *Democratic Education*, *Liberal Equality*, *Democracy and the Welfare State*, and *Ethics and Politics*. Her teaching and research interests include moral and political philosophy, practical ethics, and education. She serves on the executive board of the Association for Practical and Professional Ethics and is the Tanner Lecturer at Stanford for 1994–95. She has been a Rockefeller Fellow, Visitor at the Institute for Advanced Study, and Visiting Professor at Harvard University. She graduated from Harvard-Radcliffe College and received her M.Sc. from the London School of Economics and her Ph.D. from Harvard.

JÜRGEN HABERMAS is Professor of Philosophy at the University of Frankfurt. He is the recipient of numerous honors, including the Hegel Prize, the Sigmund Freud Prize, the Adorno Prize, and the Geschwister-Scholl Prize. His books available in English include *The Structural Transformation of the Public Sphere, Theory and Practice, Knowledge and Human Interests, Toward a Rational Society, The Theory of Communicative Action, The Philosophical Discourse of Modernity, Post-Metaphysical Thinking,* and *Between Facts and Norms* (forthcoming).

STEVEN C. ROCKEFELLER is Professor of Religion at Middlebury College, where he has served as Department Chair and Dean of the College. His research and teaching focus on the integration of democratic values, ecology, and religion. Author of *John Dewey: Religious Faith and Democratic Religious Humanism,* he is a member of the National Commission on the Environment, convened by the World Wildlife Fund. He is also President and founder of the Wendell Gilley Museum in Southwest Harbor, Maine. He has directed the interfaith symposium Spirit and Nature: Religion, Ethics, and Environmental Crisis, has spoken widely about nature, values, and spirituality, and was interviewed by Bill Moyers for "A World of Ideas." He received his B.A. from Princeton University, his M.Div. from Union Theological Seminary, and a Ph.D. from Columbia University.

CHARLES TAYLOR is Professor of Philosophy and Political Science at McGill University. He was for many years Chichele Professor of Social and Political Theory at Oxford and a fellow of All Souls College. He has also taught at Princeton, the University of California at Berkeley, and l'Université de Montreal, and has lectured at many universities around the world. His books include *The Explanation of Behavior, Hegel, Human Agency and Language, Philosophy and the Human Sciences,* and most recently *Sources of the Self.* He has published numerous articles and reviews on the philosophy of mind, psychology, and politics. He is active in politics and has run for Canadian Federal Parliament on behalf of the New Democratic party. He was recently appointed to the Conseil de la Langue Française in his native Quebec, where he takes an ongoing interest in public life.

MICHAEL WALZER is a Permanent Member of the Faculty at the School of Social Sciences at Princeton's Institute for Advanced Study. Prior to joining the Institute, he taught at Princeton and Harvard, and won a national award for excellence in teaching from the Danforth Foundation. His many books include *The Revolution of the Saints* (winner of the 1991 Benjamin E. Lippincott Award of the American Political Science Association), *Obligations, Just and Unjust*

Wars, Spheres of Justice, Interpretation and Social Criticism, and *The Company of Critics.* He is an editor of *Dissent* magazine and a contributing editor of *The New Republic,* and serves on the editorial boards of *Philosophy & Public Affairs* and *Political Theory.* He is a frequent contributor to these and many other journals. He graduated from Brandeis University and received his Ph.D. in political science from Harvard.

Susan Wolf is Professor of Philosophy at The Johns Hopkins University. She has taught at Dartmouth, Harvard, Princeton, and the University of Maryland. She is author of *Freedom Within Reason* and many articles in ethics and philosophy of mind, including "Moral Saints," "Above and Below the Line of Duty," "Sanity and the Metaphysics of Responsibility," "Ethics, Legal Ethics, and the Ethics of Law," and "The Importance of Free Will." She has been awarded fellowships from the American Council of Learned Societies and the American Association of University Women. She is a contributor to the *Journal of Philosophy, Mind,* and *Ethics,* of which she serves on the editorial board. She received her B.A. in mathematics and philosophy from Yale and her Ph.D. in philosophy from Princeton.

❖ Index ❖

abortion, 19, 22
Ackerman, Bruce, 56
affluence, 141
African-Americans: cultural identity and, 3, 4, 8–9, 77, 81, 82, 153, 154–55; curriculum and, 7–8, 13, 14, 18, 65, 79, 80; life-scripts and, 161; self-esteem and, 26, 76
"American Scholar, The," 16–17
Amish, 76, 131
Amnesty International, 64
anthropocentrism, 93, 96
anti-Semitism, 21–22
Arendt, Hannah, 15
aristocracy, 6, 27
Aristotle, 15, 16, 17
artists, 152, 153
Asian-Americans: cultural identity and, 3, 4, 8–9, 76, 81, 82; curriculum and, 13, 18, 79
assimilation, 38, 138
atomism, 7
Austria, 143
authenticity, 28–32, 34–38
Autobiography of Frederick Douglass, The, 15
autonomy, 39–40, 52–53, 57, 89, 92, 162–63; cultural, 119, 158; individual, x, xi, 112–16

barbarism, 72
Barchas, Isaac, 13
Basques, 119
Beauvoir, Simone de, 15
Bellow, Saul, 42, 71, 79–80, 83, 84
bilingualism, 52–59
bills of rights, 52–55, 59, 62–63, 100
biocentrism, 93–96, 98
Bloom, Allan, 16
Bohemian ideal, 154

Bosnia-Herzegovina, 127
Buber, Martin, 95
Buddhism, 89

Caliban, 26
California, 95
Canada: aboriginal rights in, 39–40, 41n, 52, 54; constitution of, 52–53; disintegration of, 52, 64; pluralism in, 3, 54–61, 64, 100, 101, 127–28. *See also* Quebec
Canadian Charter of Rights (1982), 52–56, 60
Canadians: aboriginal, 39–40, 41n, 52, 54; English, 4, 9, 54–56, 60, 64; French, 4, 9, 41n, 52–61, 64, 76, 89, 92, 111, 127, 157
Canadian Supreme Court, 53n, 55
Catholics, 161
censorship, 81–82
child abuse, 91
children, 158, 159
"child welfare," 115
China, 89
Christianity, 4, 9, 46, 49, 62, 77, 96, 126
citizenship: basic rights of, 4, 10–13, 37–38, 51–63, 68, 91, 92, 99, 101–3, 125; equality and, 4–8, 27, 35, 37–41, 46–51, 57–61; "first-class," 37; French, 145; German, 145; as identity, 88; liberal education and, 13–17; naturalization and, 138, 144; obligations of, 17–18; political culture and, 134; public recognition and, 46–51; "second-class," 37–39; socioeconomic status and, 38, 39, 40, 41n; and the state, 126
civil disobedience, 15
civilization, 72, 79–80, 94

169